To Kate

# PASSAGE TO GREENLAND

Best wishes

Judith Cranswick

Judith Cranswick

www.judithcranswick.co.uk

# Itinerary

| | |
|---|---|
| Day 1 | Southampton |
| Day 2 | At Sea |
| Day 3 | Kirkwall, Scotland |
| Day 4 | At Sea |
| Day 5 | At Sea |
| Day 6 | Reykjavik, Iceland |
| Day 7 | Isafjordur, Iceland |
| Day 8 | At Sea |
| Day 9 | Prince Christian Sound |
| Day 10 | At Sea |
| Day 11 | Nuuk, Greenland |
| Day 12 | At Sea |
| Day 13 | Narsarsuaq, Greenland |
| Day 14 | Nanortalik, Greenland |
| Day 15 | Qaqortoq, Greenland |
| Day 16 | At Sea |
| Day 17 | At Sea |
| Day 18 | Belfast, Northern Ireland |
| Day 19 | At Sea |
| Day 20 | At Sea |

# Day 4

At Sea

# Chapter 1

'Someone's stolen my bag!'

All eyes in the restaurant turned to look at the heavily built woman on her feet in the centre of the room. Her face was almost as red as her voluminous hand-knitted cardigan.

We were too far away to hear what the younger woman at her table was saying but it was easy to get the gist.

'Of course, I didn't leave it in the cabin. I always carry it with me.' The strident voice rang out.

The head waiter was quickly at her side but whatever he said failed to calm the situation.

'I demand to speak to the captain…'

As the ranting continued, the majority of the diners turned back to their meals and the general murmur of conversation resumed.

'Oh dear,' I said to the others sitting with me. 'I don't rate that poor man's chances.'

There was more disruption when several waiters began searching for the missing bag under the tables around the still protesting woman, much to the dismay of those being disturbed.

Over the three years that Graham had been a guest lecturer for Cygnet Cruises, we'd encountered the odd difficult passenger but this one took the prize.

'We've come across that lady before,' I said to David, the photography lecturer and his wife Gwen who had invited us to have dinner with them. 'The day we came aboard, Graham and I went up to the Ocean Café for lunch. She and her family were sitting at the next table.'

'She was complaining even then,' Graham said. 'Nothing was right. Their cabin was too far from the lifts, the buffet was crowded, and all the waiters were foreign. At the time, I put it down to the fact that they'd probably been travelling all morning. It does make some people a bit fractious.'

'That's one word for it, I suppose,' said David. 'But finding fault appears to be her modus operandi. She was on the tour in Kirkwall that I was escorting yesterday. It was a panoramic drive of the island with a few photo stops. Everything was going well until she made some very uncalled-for remarks about our guide. He was only a young chap. I presume he was on a summer break from university, but he certainly knew his stuff. He very sensibly, ignored her and carried on telling us about the Standing Stones of Stenness, but another passenger took the woman to task for constantly making snide remarks and interrupting him. The whole thing quickly became very unpleasant. In the end, I had to step in and ask everyone to stop and get back on the coach, which didn't make me too popular with those who still wanted to carry on taking photos.'

'Escorting tour groups can be a bit stressful on the rare occasion,' Graham said.

'There was an atmosphere in the coach for a while, but at the end her daughter came to apologise to both the guide and to me. It's the poor husband I feel sorry for. He always looks so frail and woebegone,' said David.

'Well let's not let the woman spoil our evening now. Shall we talk about something else?' Turning to me, Gwen asked, 'Is this your first time on board *The Sea Dream*, Amanda?'

I liked Gwen. Her Brummie accent wasn't nearly as marked as her husband's. Although we'd only known them for a few days, they seemed a pleasant, unassuming couple.

I shook my head. 'No. Graham's been booked as a guest speaker several times. How about you two?'

'Actually, this is the first time I've done anything like this.' David gave a self-effacing grin. 'It's a bit daunting up on that stage in a big theatre.'

'I don't think you need to worry, it was a great lecture,' I said. 'I'm not much of a photographer, I generally leave all that to Graham, but I do like to take a few pictures especially when Graham and I are on different tours. Getting the best out of your smartphone camera is a great idea for talks.'

I'd obviously said the right thing because he looked reassured.

'I wasn't certain how well my talks would go down with a ship's audience. Back home, I have a website and I run online photography courses but then you know the people who sign up have a genuine interest in photography.' He gave a deep frown. 'Not that many people came. The theatre was packed for the lecture on Kirkwall.'

'You shouldn't go by that. The port talks are always well attended' Graham said. 'Everyone wants to know what they can do when they go ashore. Don't forget, there's lots going on around the ship and all the lectures are recorded so that people can watch on the television in their cabins at a more convenient time. Those who came to your talk genuinely seemed to enjoy what you had to say. And lots of people came to ask you questions afterwards and that's always a good sign.'

'Have you always been a professional photographer?' I asked.

'I've been passionate about photography ever since my dad bought me my first camera for my eleventh birthday, but I've been winding down for a few years now. I don't do any more private work, but I still get asked to speak to groups and at photography conventions. And of course, there's the website.'

'When is your first lecture, Graham? You're talking about history, is that right?' asked Gwen.

'Tomorrow after lunch. It's basically about Viking exploration and the early settlement in Iceland.' He grinned at David. 'I may have a little more experience at lecturing on board ship than you, but it will still be my first time talking about history in this part of Europe. My specialist area is the classical world, so you're not the only one stepping out of their comfort zone.'

# Day 5

## At Sea

*Tomorrow we will arrive in Iceland, which is geologically the youngest country in the world, and the last one in Europe to be settled and populated.*

*Known as the land of fire and ice, it is a country of contrasts. It is one of the most volcanically active regions on earth with volcanoes, vast lava fields, hot springs and erupting geysers, yet the interior is covered with permanent icecaps which make it uninhabitable.*

*The earliest book of Icelandic history claims that Iceland was discovered by Naddoddr when he was blown off course as he sailed from Norway to the Faroes. In 870 AD a Swedish sailor, Gadar Svavrsson also accidentally drifted to the coast of Iceland. He circumnavigated the island before sailing home.*

*The first person to arrive intending to settle in Iceland was the Norwegian nicknamed Raven Floki. He spent his summer hunting seals, but because he failed to make any hay for his animals, when winter came, all the livestock he had brought with him died from starvation. Pack ice in the fjord prevented him from sailing, and by the time it finally broke up, it was too late in the year to risk trying to return to Norway. He was forced to stay for another winter. Thoroughly disillusioned, Floki decided to name the island, 'Iceland'.*

*He was followed by many other emigrant Scandinavian settlers and their Celtic slaves.*

*The Icelandic Parliament, known as the Althing, was established in 930 AD. For two weeks every summer, chieftains from across the island held an outdoor assembly on the plains of Thingvellir in order to decide on legislation. This makes the Althing the oldest parliament in the world.*

Extract from the Cygnet Daily

# Chapter 2

Graham emerged from the bathroom with a towel wrapped around his waist. Despite his age, he had managed to maintain his lean physique even if the wet hair that currently stuck up in spikes was considerably thinner than on the day that we were married over forty years ago.

Catching sight of myself in the mirror, I gave a deep sigh then quickly buttoned up a shirt long enough to cover my now bulky hips. I may have had a sylphlike figure the day I walked down the aisle, but my dress size has increased by at least three sizes in the intervening years, and no matter how hard I try to suck in my stomach, I doubted it will ever be flat again. Why is it that men like Graham can eat to their hearts content without putting on weight, whereas I only have to look at a cream cake to pile on the ounces?

The prospect of another two and a half weeks on a luxury cruise ship with all its mouth-watering temptations on offer almost twenty-four hours a day wasn't likely to improve matters. Time for some willpower. No more bacon rolls, croissants or Danish pastries for breakfast. Just fresh fruit with perhaps one slice of toast. And definitely no afternoon tea. I love the whole ceremony of it – not to mention the finger sandwiches, three-tiered cake stands with bite-sized macaroons, eclairs, chocolate brownies, fondant sponges, almond slices, topped off with warm scones piled high with oodles of clotted cream and jam.

My good resolution was beginning to falter by lunchtime. I stuck to a bowl of soup and a tuna salad, then succumbed to a crusty roll with each of them. Luckily, I was spared the temptation of dessert as Graham's lecture was straight after lunch, so we had to be back in the cabin for him to get changed to go up on stage.

'I can't find my keycard,' I said as I rummaged through the assorted clutter on the dressing table.

Graham stood in the doorway, changing his laptop from one hand to the other trying not to make a point of looking at his watch.

'When did you have it last?'

He was always apprehensive before giving a lecture, and being an understanding, supportive wife, I refrained from snapping back the obvious. I forced a smile.

'Don't wait for me, darling. You go down and get set up. I'll join you in a second.'

He hesitated for just long enough to be polite then headed down the corridor, letting the door swing closed behind him.

'Thanks for stating the flaming obvious. If I knew when I last used the blasted thing it wouldn't be lost, would it?' I muttered. I'm not that long-suffering!

I pulled open the top drawer and rifled through the contents. It wasn't on my bedside table either. I searched the floor. Even under the bed. The only other possible place was in a cardigan or trouser pocket. The hangers jangled as I thrust my way through the contents of my end of the tiny wardrobe sending blouses cascading to the floor.

'This is getting ridiculous!'

I took a deep breath and tried to think logically.

Had I taken it up to lunch? I must have done. I never leave the cabin without it. I could vaguely remember putting my hand in my pocket to get it out as we came back down the stairs. But Graham had used his card when we'd reached our cabin door. Then my mind went blank.

I sat on the bed and closed my eyes, trying to picture myself coming through the door. What did I do next?

I'd gone to the bathroom.

Success. It was on the floor by the toilet. It must have fallen out of my pocket when I went to the loo.

I let out a long sigh of relief and stared at my red face in the mirror. My hair was all over the place. Perhaps I should put some makeup on and make myself more presentable. There was still plenty of time. Graham's lecture wouldn't start for a good half hour.

Probably best not to put any more pressure on him. I raked a comb through my short grey bob – the Covid lockdown had been a good excuse to stop the tedious routine of dyeing my hair – and headed out.

Graham always insisted that we take the stairs when we were on the ship as we needed the exercise, but the number showing above the nearest lift indicated that it was at our deck level. It made sense to save time.

I pressed the button. The doors slid open.

A woman lay slumped in the far corner, legs akimbo, unblinking, wide eyes staring blindly into nothingness.

Just how long I stood there before I could force my inert body into action, I have no idea. Probably no more than a couple of seconds. I hurried forward and knelt on one knee to put two fingers on her neck. I knew it was pointless. Although the flesh was still warm, the staring eyes told me everything I needed to know.

It had been less than three months since I'd renewed my first aid training certificate and I realised I was already doing things in the wrong order. Her head was thrown back, so her airway was clear. Check for breathing. I put my cheek to her open lips. Nothing. Was there any point trying CPR? Even if there had been, there was no way I could start pumping her chest where she was propped half-curled against the wall without first getting her body flat on the floor. She was a big woman, a good four or five inches taller than me and heavily overweight. There was no way I had the strength to move her.

I tried shouting for help but there was no response. Not that I'd expected any as I'd seen no one about earlier. Best to take her straight to the medical centre down in the depths of the ship. I scrambled to my feet and punched the bottom button.

Though I had never been down that far before, I knew the medical centre was at the stern of the ship. As soon as the lift doors slid open, I yelled at the top of my voice. My cries were answered almost immediately. A nurse came bustling out of the door almost opposite.

'I found her like this...'

Ignoring me, the nurse shouted over her shoulder, 'Doctor, doctor!'

I was pushed aside but before I had a chance to escape, the doctor and a second nurse appeared, and I found myself squeezed into the opposite corner of the lift trying not to get in the way.

Someone brought a defibrillator. I watched as the doctor unceremoniously took hold of her legs and yanked the body forward until it was lying flat so that the leads could be attached to her chest.

Not that it did any good. After ten minutes, the woman was declared dead.

The doctor knelt back and with a resigned sigh said, 'Let's get the body into the surgery.'

'I'll get a stretcher.' The male nurse was the first to get to his feet.

Time for me to escape. I hovered in the corridor uncertain if I should leave or not. I was clearly surplus to requirements.

'Heart attack?' queried one of the nurses.

'But what about the blood?' My voice was barely above a whisper.

The doctor looked at me with a frown and I pointed to the long smear of blood on the back wall that had revealed when the body had been pulled forward.

He shrugged his shoulders. 'She probably hit the back of

her head when she collapsed.'

I couldn't decide if that was what he genuinely believed or had decided that the cause of death should not be discussed in front of the likes of me. Either way, it was clearly time for me to go.

I looked around trying to get my bearings. The medical centre was at the back of the ship at the far end of a wide corridor with bare steel walls.

The door at the far end of the corridor suddenly banged open. A tall, barrel-chested man strode towards us, his heels clicking loudly on the uncarpeted floor. The lower deck had none of the comfort of the passenger areas, but then few passengers ever ventured into what was essentially crew domain.

'Captain,' acknowledged the doctor and proceeded to explain the situation to the newcomer.

'Where was the body found?' asked the captain.

'This lady brought her down in the lift.'

The captain turned to glare at me.

'And you are?'

'My name is Amanda Mitchell. I discovered her in the lift and brought her straight down here.'

'Do you know who she is?'

'No, Captain. Not by name, but she is the woman who lost her handbag last night. I believe she's travelling with her husband, daughter, and son-in-law.'

'I see.' He turned back to the doctor.

I assumed that was my cue to leave and beat a hurried retreat.


It came as a surprise when I looked at my watch to discover that Graham's lecture had not yet begun. This whole dreadful business which had seemed to take up the entire afternoon had lasted less than half an hour.

The theatre was almost full by the time I made my way down to the front of the auditorium to where Graham was standing at the foot of the stage steps. He was busy talking to Kirsten the cruise director, an elegant, slim woman with a permanent smile. He turned and smiled at me as I took my seat on the front row.

'Sorry I'm late,' I mouthed.

Moments later, the two went up onto the stage. The lights dimmed and I slumped down in my seat taking deep breaths trying to steady my nerves. I'd been so incensed by the way the captain had made me feel as though I was some kind of voyeur who snuck into something that did not concern me, that only now did the full horror of what I'd witnessed began to sink in. All I could think about was the poor woman's body sliding down the back wall as it was dragged to the floor and the long thick smear of blood that it left behind. The memory sent a shiver down my spine.

It wasn't just the words of Kirsten's introduction that washed over me. It was only when the applause started and the lights went up, that I realised that Graham's entire lecture was all over. By the time he'd removed his microphone and packed away his laptop, a small queue of people had gathered by the stage steps eager to ask him questions. I pushed myself to my feet.

I must have stood up too quickly because I suddenly felt quite nauseous. A quick exit wasn't possible as I had to follow the slow-moving mass of people making their way out of the theatre. There was a small crush of people waiting for the lifts, but I managed to squeeze past to the stairs without too much difficulty.

Our cabin was almost at the end of the corridor, and it was with a huge sense of relief that I managed to make it to the bathroom in time.

I was still there ten minutes later when I heard the door open.

'Amanda?'

'In here.'

I splashed water onto my face then caught sight of my drained countenance in the mirror as I lifted my head. My hair was a mess. I ran my fingers through it, patted it into some semblance of order and went to join him.

Graham was unpacking his laptop at the dressing table which he'd commandeered as his workstation.

'Well, that went down well, I thought,' he said, the tension visibly easing from his shoulders.

'You certainly had lots of people come to chat at the end.'

'I take it you found your keycard in the end.' He turned to look at me. 'My goodness. You look like death warmed up. Are you okay?'

'Not really.' I sank down onto the end of the bed and poured out the story in a none too coherent fashion.

'You poor, poor love.' He sat down beside me and put an arm around my shoulder pulling me close.

The unexpected knock at the door made me jump.

# Chapter 3

'May I speak to Mrs Mitchell?'

Though I couldn't see him – I was still sitting on the bed – I recognised the captain's voice straightaway and pushed myself to my feet.

'You'd better come in, sir.'

Graham held the door open letting the captain precede him. At six-foot-one, Graham can hardly be considered a small man and he is no weakling, but the captain towered over him with wide shoulders to match.

'Good evening, Mrs Mitchell. This was found on the floor of the lift, and we were wondering if it belongs to you.'

He held out my Kindle.

'Thank you. I must have dropped it in all the confusion. I hadn't even realised it was missing. I usually take it with me down to the theatre to read while Graham's getting ready for his lecture.' Quite why I was gabbling about nothing like some gauche adolescent, I had no idea. The captain had that effect on me.

'Actually, while I'm here, I would like a word with you both.' He strode to the sitting area in front of the balcony windows and waved us to the two easy chairs.

Once we were seated, he took the upright chair tucked under the dressing table and turned it round for himself.

'As the guest lecturer and partner, I am sure you will appreciate that it is part of your contract to uphold the good name of the company and to be discreet while you are on board. Therefore, Mrs Mitchell, I would ask you not to mention finding the body of that poor woman to any of the passengers. Obviously, it will be impossible to keep her death a secret, but nonetheless, it is beholden on you both not to discuss this matter with anyone.'

We both nodded and Graham muttered, 'Understood, captain.'

The captain turned to me. 'As you will appreciate, after any accident or incident onboard there is a great deal of red tape, including paperwork to complete. As you found the body, Mrs Mitchell, we will require you to make a brief statement. If you would be good enough to go down to the security office before you go to dinner this evening, it would be much appreciated.'

With that he got to his feet, gave a slight dip of the head, wished us both good evening and marched to the door.

Once he'd gone, Graham looked at me and raised an eyebrow. 'Well, he was a right barrel of laughs.'

Despite the way I was feeling, I had to smile. 'He does have a knack of making you feel like a naughty schoolchild.'

'I wouldn't say that. He's just a pompous nobody who likes to wear a uniform to lord it over everyone else.'

'Can't argue with that.' I gave a deep sigh. 'However, no sense putting it off. I'd better go down and get it over with.'

He took my arm in his. 'No! Right now, you and I are going down to the main lounge to have a nice cup of tea. You need a quiet sit down and to recover your equilibrium before you even think of tackling anything else. Doctor's orders.'

Although we regularly cruised on *The Sea Dream* and its two sister ships, we rarely ate in the luxuriously furnished main restaurant by choice. Its dark crimson swagged curtains and heavy mahogany chairs and serving stands gave it a somewhat claustrophobic atmosphere. We much preferred the more open feel of the less formal restaurant known as the Ocean Café on one of the upper decks, which has floor to ceiling windows all down each side.

At half past six in the evening, the place was almost empty, and we had a table to ourselves by the window. Although I was feeling much more my usual self, I still wasn't in the mood for being particularly sociable.

'Something wrong with the fish?' Graham asked when I put down my knife and fork and pushed away my plate.

I shook my head. 'I'm just not that hungry tonight. I keep thinking about that poor woman.'

'Have you any idea who she was?'

I pulled a face. 'The woman who lost her handbag at dinner yesterday.'

'The one who kept complaining all the time?'

'That's the one.'

He grimaced. 'If you ask me, she was a heart attack waiting to happen.'

'Graham!'

'Well,' he said, sheepishly, 'You have to admit, she didn't do much to make herself popular.'

'Perhaps not. But the poor woman is dead when all is said and done. Besides, I don't think it was a heart attack.'

'What are you saying? You're not suggesting she was murdered?' He gave a wry laugh.

When I said nothing, he stared at me for a moment. 'Amanda?'

'I'm not saying that, exactly,' I answered. 'But there was something strange about her death. I'm not convinced that the blood on the lift wall was because she banged her head when she fell.'

He raised his eyebrows. 'You've been reading too many crime novels, old girl.'

He was too busy holding up an empty wine glass trying to catch the waiter's eye to notice my expression.

Don't misunderstand me, I love him dearly, but there are times when my husband can be a patronising git. To make it worse he doesn't even realise that he's doing it. Being treated like one of his students who has just given a silly answer to one of his questions doesn't sit well with me. He may have climbed a lot higher up the career ladder than I ever did, but then he hadn't had to take eight years out to bring up our children.

The last thing I wanted was to make a scene especially where we could be overheard by the other passengers, so I bit my tongue. For the rest of the meal, I let him prattle on listening with only half an ear whilst I thought about what was wrong with the way the dead woman was lying in the lift when I found her.

# Day 6

*Reykjavik, Iceland*

*Reykjavik is the most northern capital of any sovereign state in the world. It is also Iceland's largest city. It is the location of the first permanent settlement established by the Vikings and became a trading post in the eighteenth century.*

*According to legend, the first permanent Scandinavian settler was Ingólfr Arnarson, a Viking chieftain who decided to leave Norway and settle in Iceland following a blood feud. He arrived in 874.*

*It was the custom for Vikings to throw two carved wooden pillars – the symbols of his office – into the sea so that the gods would show settlers where they should set up their new home. Arnason's pillars came ashore in present-day Reykjavík, so he settled there with his family.*

Extract from the Cygnet Daily

# Chapter 4

I woke in the early hours and lay there for some time before falling asleep again just as day light began to peep round the edges of the curtains. It was probably the sound of splashing water coming from the bathroom that woke me. Graham was already up and in the shower. I stretched out in the enormous bed and despite the restless night, felt surprisingly perky.

'Morning,' I said brightly when he appeared.

I threw back the covers and nipped into the bathroom.

Neither of us had been asked to escort a tour so there was no rush, but there was no point in wasting the day either. We left the cabin and walked towards the stairs.

'Someone's not happy,' said Graham, as we heard angry complaints coming from the landing. We turned the corner to see eight or so people were crowded round the doors of the far lift.

An overweight, round-faced man was angrily punching the call button. 'It's been stuck on the top deck for ages. What the heck are they doing up there? We've been waiting here for ten minutes.'

'Don't exaggerate, Ken. Be a bit more patient. With the other lift out of order, it's bound to take a bit more time.'

A cold chill ran down my spine as I looked up at the illuminated sign above the lift that read OUT OF SERVICE. I knew the reason why.

Graham's hand took mine and he gently tugged me away to the stairs. We walked up together. As we reached the top of the first flight, he gave my hand a reassuring squeeze. He seemed to know instinctively what I was thinking and feeling. He kept hold of my hand all the way to the top floor. Normally, he would take the stairs two at a time, waiting for me at the top while I struggled up the last few flights. By the time we'd mounted all hundred odd stairs, I'd forced myself to push away all thoughts of yesterday's gruesome discovery and recovered sufficiently to give him a smile and a thank you hand squeeze. I didn't risk saying anything out loud in case he started talking about it.

The Ocean Café was far from crowded when we walked in, but then it was just after nine o'clock, and many people had already left the ship on one of the shore excursions.

'Margaret is sitting on her own over there. Shall we go and join her?'

Graham gave me a puzzled look. 'She's the port lecturer's wife,' I muttered.

'Hi there, may we join you?'

'Please do.' She moved her bag from the chair beside her, and I sat down while Graham went to get himself some cereal from the buffet. 'I'm on my own. Paul's already left. He's escorting the Golden Circle tour. It's an eight-hour trip so he won't be back till late. They've asked me to escort the included excursion around Reykjavik which doesn't leave till 11. What are you two doing today?'

'It's a free day for us. We've been to Reykjavik before many years ago on a land tour with the children, so we decided to catch the shuttle bus to the centre when we're ready and have a mooch around and perhaps visit a couple of museums.'

'Lucky you,' she said with feeling.

'Don't you like escorting?'

'It's not that. Though I can't say I find it much fun especially if it's a big group. And there's a lot of walking involved on this one. I'm always worried someone is going to get lost. Plus, I'm so busy trying to keep an eye on the guests that I miss all the sights anyway. I seem to spend all my time chivvying along the stragglers and when we do catch up with the rest of the group, the guide is already halfway through their spiel.'

'You don't have to do it. It is voluntary.'

'I know, but Paul always says it gets him a few brownie points. The more helpful you are, the more likely the company will invite you back.' She gave a long sigh. 'It's just that Paul and I don't seem to get much time to spend together on his lecture cruises. It's not like a proper holiday. Take yesterday when we were in Kirkwall. Paul went to the Italian Chapel, but I wasn't needed so I stayed on board all day.'

'Why didn't you catch the shuttle bus into the centre and have a look round by yourself?'

'We were in Kirkwall a couple of months ago on a Norway cruise. We went all around the cathedral, the castle and the little museum so there didn't seem much point in going again on my own.'

'Couldn't you have booked onto the Italian Chapel excursion as a paying passenger and gone with him?'

'I did try, but it was fully booked.'

I smiled sympathetically. 'That's the trouble with lecturing. We can't book tours until we get on board by which time there are no seats left on the coach especially on the more popular ones. It would be a help if we had some idea of when we'd be needed to escort in advance, but things never seem to be sorted until the day before when it's often too late to book anything else anyway.'

It was hard work trying to jolly her along, and I was quite relieved when Graham returned, and it was my turn to go and get something to eat. She had disappeared by the time I got back.

'Margaret said to give you her regards. She's gone to get ready.'

'Not a very happy little bunny!'

'Oh?'

'With Paul being so busy all the time, I get the impression

the poor woman feels a bit of a spare part.'

He put down his teacup and frowned. 'You don't feel like that do you?'

'Of course not. I admit escorting duties can be a bit tedious at times, but I enjoy going on trips, especially to places I haven't seen before and meeting new people. And on the days when we're at sea, I'm more than happy catching up with my reading and chatting to other passengers in one of the lounges when you're busy. Margaret strikes me as a timid little thing, and it doesn't come naturally to just sit down and start talking with strangers.'

The shuttle bus dropped us off outside the massive Harpa Concert Hall and Conference Centre which was supposed to be one of the major landmarks of Reykjavik.

'Can't say I'm impressed,' said Graham as we stared up at the towering building whose square walls consisted of solid rows of black-tinted windows.'

'It is a bit oppressive. Perhaps it looks better with the sun shining on it.'

'Humph! Looked spectacular enough in the photos that Paul showed in his port talk.'

'True, but they were taken at night when the windows were lit up in all different colours.' I tucked my arm through his. 'Besides, isn't it the job of the destinations lecturer to make everywhere sound as wonderful as possible?'

We headed first to the Harllgrimskirkya, the Lutheran Church in the heart of the city. It wasn't long before we could see the thin pointed spire soaring up in the distance. The architecture was very unusual for a church. It consisted of a series of thin symmetrical columns rising steeply to the centre. According to Paul's lecture, it was intended to represent the basalt lava which underpins Iceland. As expected, the interior was equally stark.

In the large square in front of the church was an enormous statue of Leif Eriksson said to be the first man to discover America long before Christopher Columbus. Graham spent the next ten minutes trying to get a decent shot. Not an easy task because it was on top of a huge pedestal-shaped like the prow of a ship. I've long since resigned myself to the amount of time Graham spends taking photos when we're out together, especially when he wants to use them to illustrate one of his history lectures. I couldn't find a bench and ended up perching against the base of another of the monuments until he'd taken shots from every angle. My thoughts drifted back to Margaret. She had my sympathy. She was probably even more of a "photography widow" than I was.

Graham was keen to go to the Settlement Exhibition which was an underground museum built around a 9th century longhouse, so we made that our next stop. I confess I found the re-creations and the digital interactive displays just as fascinating as he did. But then history was my subject too. That was how we first met – studying for the same degree at university.

'I need a coffee and a sit down after all that,' I said when we eventually came out.

'Me too. You'd have thought a place that large would have had its own café.'

We searched the nearby streets, but at least in that quarter of the city, coffee shops appeared to be non-existent.

'Time's getting on,' he said. 'How about we make our way back down to the harbour area? We're bound to pass something.'

We did come across several restaurants, but none of them would serve us coffee unless we ordered a meal, which we didn't want.

'Do you think the Saga Museum will have its own café?' I asked.

'Wouldn't bank on it.'

The Saga Museum took us through a series of life-sized dioramas and models of Icelandic Vikings using an audio guide. Graham had the opportunity to take more photos to illustrate future lectures, but, as he had predicted, we drew a blank on the café.

We left the museum soon after three o'clock. There was still plenty of time before the last shuttlebus back to the ship but by now we were both not only thirsty, but brain dead and much as we'd both enjoyed the day, neither of us could face the thought of another museum.

'Back to the ship?'

I nodded.

By the time we arrived back at the Harpa Concert Hall, there was already a small queue for the shuttlebus. As we stood waiting, it was impossible not to overhear the conversation going on in front of us.

'It turned into a right old dingdong. She stood up, leant across the table shaking her fist in his face, calling him every name under the sun. Everyone in the lounge turned to look. It was really embarrassing.'

Graham and I looked at each other with raised eyebrows.

'So, what did he do then?'

'He gave as good as he got, believe you me! Said she was an ungrateful cow and if she didn't learn to keep her vile tongue in check, he'd shut her up for good. Then he stormed out with a face like thunder. Her face was as red as a beetroot. I'm surprised she didn't drop down with a heart attack there and then.'

'Here comes the coach!' cried Graham, in a loud voice and the gossip came to an end as everyone cheered and turned to look.


The Atrium Lounge on the main deck is the focal point of the ship. Situated between the shops and the reception area, it's a popular place to have a tea or coffee at any time of the day. There is also a counter which serves cookies, small cakes and ice cream. At four o'clock every afternoon, waiters appear with trolleys laden with scones, jam and two different types of cream. Needless to say, by the time that we arrived back on the ship, the place was crowded. All the easy chairs were taken, but, as we hovered looking for somewhere to sit, a couple got up and vacated a small table in a far corner.

'You grab a seat and I'll go and get us a scone. Clotted cream for you?'

'Need you ask?'

I wasted no time and only just beat another couple to the empty table. Much to my surprise, a waitress appeared to take away the dirty crockery and take our order almost straight away.

'I asked for a pot of tea. Hope that's alright with you,' I said, when Graham eventually came back.

'Fine.'

We had almost finished, Graham was licking the last of the sticky jam from his fingers, when I noticed something was happening at the entrance onto the gangway. Several of the crew had gathered and were waiting expectantly.

'Something's up,' I said.

Before Graham could comment, the captain appeared, accompanied by one of the senior officers.

'Looks like someone important is coming aboard.'

A fair-haired man dressed in a three-piece suit, a heavy coat over one arm and pulling a modest-sized wheeled suitcase behind him, appeared in the doorway. The captain stepped forward holding out his hand. We were too far away to hear what was being said, but after an initial greeting, the stranger was led away followed by a member of the crew pulling the newcomer's case.

Graham and I looked at each other with raised eyebrows.

'I don't know who that was, but I very much doubt that it was one of the new entertainers.'

'Like to hazard a guess?' he asked.

I gave a sigh. 'Something tells me, he must have something to do with the dead woman.'

# Day 7

*Isafjordur Iceland*

*Isafjordur lies in the far northeast corner of Iceland, tucked away inside an arm of the fjord jutting out with steep mountains rising dramatically on three sides. Established by Danish traders in the eighteenth century, the original village grew to become the country's major fishing port for centuries. When industry declined, so did its population – to almost half, and the economy has been forced to diversify. Tourism has made an important contribution in recent years.*

Extract from the Cygnet Daily

# Chapter 5

The cabin stewards leave a copy of the Cygnet Daily – a double page spread which gives details of the next day's events – in each cabin when they turn down the beds and tidy the bathrooms in the evening. We usually look through it when we get back after dinner. Because we had gone straight from our meal to the theatre and then had a drink in the bar with a couple of people we'd got talking to the previous night, neither of us had had time to read it before we went to bed. I decided to take it up with us when we went for breakfast.

I was busy reading it when Graham suddenly said. 'It's a pity about that other cruise ship getting here ahead of us.'

'Sorry?'

He pointed to the ship lying in the small dock in the distance. 'That's why we've had to anchor out here in the fjord.'

'Oh yeah. I hadn't noticed. I knew we were going to be using the ship's tenders to go ashore. Do you think any of those big cruise ships ever come in here?'

'I shouldn't think so. The town's population is only two and a half thousand. The place would be swamped.'

'One good thing about being out here in the fjord is that you get a fantastic view of the shoreline and the old town with the mountain slopes behind,' I said.

'It is quite impressive, especially with the snow on the peaks. I think I'll fetch my camera and pop up to the observation deck after breakfast and take a few pictures while the sun's still shining. You never know, it might have gone by the time we get back.' He popped the last of his croissant into his mouth and chewed appreciatively before continuing, 'What time's your excursion?'

'I have to be in the theatre at eight o'clock.'

'The botanical garden and the village tour leaves fifteen minutes later but I should be back by lunchtime so we can have lunch together. How about we go ashore again in the afternoon and have a mosey around the place. It looks quite attractive.'

'Great idea,' I agreed. 'If Paul's port talk is anything to go by, there's quite a bit to see.'


Tour escorts are expected to be in the theatre at least a quarter of an hour before the passengers are supposed to assemble. The trip to see the arctic foxes inevitably proved popular and there were to be two coaches going. It was billed as an easy tour with little walking and only a few steps, which meant it ought to be a straightforward one for me.

I only recognised a couple of faces as I guided my group to the allotted rows of seats in the theatre, but I always like to make a special note of the people who had come on their own to help ensure they don't feel isolated from the rest of the group. As we would be spending most of the time either at the Artic Fox Research Centre or in the community hall in the same village, I couldn't see that being a problem.

It was a surprise to discover that our guide, a young man in his late twenties, was English. He introduced himself as Philip and explained that he'd come to do a research project for his PhD in marine biology at the University Centre. He'd fallen in love with the place and had decided to stay.

'Did you give it all up to be a tour guide?' someone asked.

He smiled and shook his head. 'Only for six weeks or so. Our tourist season is very short, especially up here in the north. My main job is in the research centre here in Isafjordur.'

The coach skirted the curve at the head inlet and along

the coast road to the south. The scenery was spectacular, and everyone had their cameras out.

'Look,' Philip pointed a little lower down the fjord ahead of us, 'There's another blow. Can you see it? It's a fin whale, you can tell from the shape of the blow.'

My seat was on the far side of the coach near the back. Everyone on my side was on their feet craning for a view making it impossible for me to see anything.

Before long the coach began to climb a steep path towards a mountain pass that would take us to the village of Sudavik on the north shore of the neighbouring inlet.

There were a great many oohs and aahs outside the artic fox enclosure. The was only the single female occupant but she was as cute and endearing as any other small furry creature.

'Don't you just want to pick her up and cuddle her?'

I laughed. 'I think you might get a nasty bite if you tried. She may have been here from when she was a tiny cub but she's far from a domestic pet.'

'It's such a shame that she's all on her own though, don't you think?' The woman sounded wistful.

'The warden did say that because she had always been fed, she would never survive in the wild having to hunt for her food. And if they introduced another fox, the two would tear each other apart. Even in the wild, they live solitary lives coming together only to mate when the female comes into season.'

Ten minutes later most people had gone to look round the small exhibition centre. I lingered to keep an eye on the elderly woman standing by the wooden fox house apart from the others. Before long she was the only one left.

Her bright royal blue padded jacket stood out and I'd noticed her sitting on her own in the bus. I waited a minute or so longer, then wandered over to her.

'Aren't you getting cold out here?'

She gave a start and looked around as if only now aware that everyone else had gone.'

'Sorry, dear. I was in a daydream.'

She pulled off one of her sky blue, knitted gloves and wiped her wet cheek with the back of her hand before tucking a stray whisp of grey hair beneath the matching bobble hat.

'Is everything alright?'

'I'm fine.' She gave me a broad smile. 'Don't mind me. I was just thinking how much my husband would have loved to see this.'

'He's not with you?'

'We booked this holiday almost a year ago, but he died quite suddenly not that long after. I was all for cancelling but my children persuaded me not to. They said he would be cross with me if I did and it's true.' Another tear escaped down her cheek. She unzipped her bulging shoulder bag and, clutching her camera, loose glove and the strap in one hand, she rooted around inside with the other. 'I know I had a pack of tissues in here.'

It was inevitable that things would fall out. I bent to pick up the fallen glove, a packet of polo mints and a passport.

'You really ought to leave this in the safe in your cabin,' I said handing back the passport. 'You don't need it when you go ashore, at least not anywhere on this cruise, and it would be disastrous if you lost it.'

'Yes, I know. But this isn't actually mine.'

'Oh?'

Her pale cheeks flushed a bright pink, and she licked her lips. 'You'll think me very silly. It's my husband's. I thought if I brought it with me, it's as though he was here enjoying all these wonderful new places with me. I mean a passport is who you are… An identity.'

'That's not silly at all. I think it's a lovely idea.'

I put an arm around her and guided her back inside as she brushed away the last of her tears.

'You know, I was in two minds about coming on my own. But I'm so pleased I did. Everyone has been so kind. The crew can't do enough for you and it's such a lovely ship.

And there must be a whole army of people keeping everywhere so spick and span. Not just the cabins. Nearly every time I go down the stairs there's a cleaner polishing the handrails. The cleaning goes on twenty-four-seven when all the passengers are tucked up in their beds.'

'Now how would you know that?'

She looked a little sheepish. 'I don't sleep too well at night, especially since Jim died. Last night I woke up around two o'clock and tossed and turned for a good hour. I tried reading but I still couldn't drop off so I decided to go down and get myself a cup of hot chocolate to see if that would help. My cabin is not far from the front stairwell but when I went to use the lift there was a man standing in the corridor in front of the landing who stopped me and told me to use the lifts at the back of the ship. He said they were cleaning the carpet.'

'I'm surprised no one complained about being woken up by the noise of the hoovers.'

She shook her head. 'They weren't vacuuming. I think they must have been shampooing it. Or about to, because all the lights were out in the stairwell.'

'I'm surprised they switch those ones off because the lights in the corridors are left on all night. I've noticed it shining under the door when I have to get up for the loo.'

'Now you mention it, it was odd. Especially as there must have been people on the landing already because I could hear them talking.'

'Perhaps there was a problem with the electricity circuit, and the men were waiting for the power to be switched on again before they could start work.'

She gave me a beaming smile. 'I expect you're right, dear.'

'It's getting cold standing out here. Shall we go in?'

We wandered round the exhibition centre together looking at all the models. Rosemary turned out to be a talkative soul. By the time we were all ready to board the coach again, I'd learnt all about her two sons and her daughter and her numerous grandchildren.

Over lunch, Graham and I exchanged notes on our respective tours and discovered that each of the villages we visited had been devastated by avalanches.

'The film they showed us in the village hall about it was an eyeopener. People came from all over Iceland to help the rescue party. Sudavik was rebuilt but even after nearly thirty years, many of the temporary wooden houses sent from Denmark and Norway are still being used.'

'It's amazing how people pull together,' Graham said. 'The same thing happened at Flateyri. We didn't have a film, but the guide told us all about it and we did see this huge A-shaped protection dam on the hillside that was built as a result of the disaster. It proved pretty effective because it deflected a second avalanche a few years later.'

I drank the last of my cappuccino and looked at my watch. 'There's a tender leaving in ten minutes, if we make a move now, we might just catch it.'

We spent the afternoon looking round the museum housed in four eighteenth century renovated buildings that were once part of the original Danish trading centre. Seeing how the people, especially the fishermen, forged an existence in the harsh conditions proved fascinating and it left us little time to explore the rest of the town.

It had been a good day. After seeing the adorable arctic fox, a pleasant gentle afternoon with Graham and an enjoyable classical concert from the string quartet after dinner, I lay my head on the pillow without the feeling of dread that had haunted my previous couple of nights when the picture of the dead body in the lift kept creeping into my mind as I lay there in the dark with no other distractions to drive it away.

The sheer horror of the scene was at last beginning to fade.

But not the sense of compulsion to discover exactly how and why she had died.

# Day 8

**At Sea**

# Chapter 6

Graham wasn't a regular churchgoer, but apart from the odd pointed comment about not being able to have a long lie in and a leisurely breakfast, he was happy enough to come with me to the Sunday service whenever we were at sea.

'At least the chaplain kept his sermon short and sweet,' he muttered as we filed out of the Ocean Lounge when it came to an end.

'It was rather brief, but I don't suppose a cruise ship is the place for a deep and meaningful analysis of theological truths.'

'The hymn singing was a bit of a disaster. The poor piano player had to start again when no one came in on cue the first time. If it hadn't been for that chap in the front row with a good strong voice, I don't know what would have happened.'

'It was a bit strange. Usually, the chaplain starts everyone off, but he didn't start singing till the last verse.

To judge from the snatches of conversation I overheard from the people following us out, Graham and I were not the only ones who had found the morning's service somewhat unusual.

'He didn't even distribute communion!' The woman's voice rose in protest.

I didn't catch her husband's more muted response, but silently I had to agree with her. There had been one occasion when things were getting back to normal after COVID that communion was stopped as a precautionary measure, but that was when we were still having daily lateral flow tests on board. Whatever the reason the Rev. Parker Scott had decided to cut out that part of the service, he had given no explanation to the congregation.

'I grant you that, but you have to admit, he's very good-looking,' came a second female voice.

'And doesn't he know it!' came the quick retort. 'And why doesn't he wear his dog collar around the ship?'

'Well, I don't suppose it's compulsory unless they are actually giving a service.'

'Maybe, but have you ever seen the ship's chaplain without his dog collar on any other cruise.' The first woman was not to be mollified.

She had a point. The Rev. Parker Scott hadn't even worn one at the guest speakers and entertainers' get-together meeting on the first evening. I hadn't been able to work out who he was until the cruise director had asked us all to introduce ourselves.

'What do you want to do now?' Graham's question brought me back from my reverie. 'I think I'll go back to the cabin and have a quick run through of the next presentation for this afternoon, if that's okay with you. Are you going to the lecture?'

'Not sure. Do you remember whose it is?' He shook his head. 'I'll come up with you and take a look at today's events sheet.'

When I looked at the programme, I discovered the lecture was on the dramatic effects of climate change in Greenland and decided to give it a miss. The last thing I needed was more doom and gloom. I'd met Dr Sybil Adams, a short plump woman with straight iron-grey hair and no-nonsense manner, at the introductory meeting. Her first lecture on the changing pattern of tides was not as dire as I had feared, but I found the topic itself far from riveting.

Armed with my Kindle and a copy of that day's sudoku, I went up to the library. Apart from an elderly gentleman getting himself a drink from the coffee station, the place was deserted. Presumably most people were either at the lecture, the craft class, or taking part in the quiz in the Ocean Lounge on the top deck. I settled myself in a high button-backed armchair facing out to sea. That day's sudoku proved to be more difficult than anticipated and it was only when it was almost complete that I realised I had gone wrong. I couldn't be bothered to go down to reception and get another copy, so I picked up my Kindle. The trouble was I'd finished the novel I'd been reading. It had been a gripping story and had me turning the pages long after Graham had switched out his bedside light and settled down to sleep. The consequence of finishing a good book is finding something interesting to replace it. I switched on my Kindle and flicked through the directory, but nothing caught my fancy. I wanted something light and undemanding.

The library is arranged with tall shelves dividing the room into small relatively secluded sections. I heard someone come in and drop heavily onto one of the couches behind me. To judge from the angry mutterings, they were clearly not in the best of moods and obviously unaware that they were not alone. Too embarrassed to make my presence known, I stared out to sea wondering how long I would be trapped.

A voice cried out, 'It's all so bloody unfair!'

Without warning, a book suddenly sailed through the air missing my chair by inches. It hit the window with a resounding crash making me jump to my feet.

I doubt he heard my cry. When I turned to look for the culprit, the man was sitting with his head in his hands rocking back and forth.

'Are you alright?' I'd said it before I could stop myself.

He looked up at me, eyes wide with shock.

'I'm so sorry. I... I didn't realise anyone else was here,' he said, haltingly.

'If you'd rather be alone, I'll go.'

It was only then that I realised who he was. Not that I knew his name, but I recognised him as one of the dead woman's relatives. 'Losing your mother-in-law suddenly like that, must have been a terrible shock.'

'Bloody woman! Still causing trouble even though she's dead.' When he saw my look of surprise, he shook his head. 'Forgive me. I'm just so wound up. Please don't let me drive you away. I'm the one who should be leaving.'

I had the feeling that he needed to talk to someone. I sank down on the settee beside him.

'By all accounts, it sounds as if she was quite a difficult woman.'

'Difficult! That's only the half of it. He clamped his mouth shut, biting back the stream of resentment clearly bursting to get out.

I let the silence hang for a long minute. 'Why don't we get a coffee, and we can talk about it? Or not.'

After only a moment's pause, he nodded. 'I am rather dry.'

I led the way to the self-service coffee station and picked up a mug. 'What would you like?'

Once we had our drinks, we returned to the settee.

'She was causing trouble before we even got on the ship, he said. 'There was a problem with one of the machines when we were going through the security check in the terminal building. Several people were asked to unpack their bags and put them through the x-ray machine again. The trays all became jammed together at the far end and things became a bit chaotic with everyone crowding in to get their stuff. That's when Doreen had a right up-and-downer with another passenger. Something to do with one of them picking up the wrong passport, I think. I kept well out of it.'

He placed his mug on the table, leant forward, elbows on his knees, staring down at his hands. 'I knew from the beginning that this cruise was a bad idea. I should never have agreed to come.'

'So why did you?'

'It was meant to be a birthday treat for Bill. It's his

eightieth this year, and Julie and her brothers wanted to give him something special. He's not been too well lately and he's getting frail. It's always been his dream to visit Greenland to see the icebergs, so they clubbed together and paid for their parents to come on a cruise.'

'That was very generous.'

He pulled a face. 'It cost a bomb. Bill is quite doddery now and he and Doreen couldn't really manage the trip on their own. Both William and George had commitments, so Julie and I agreed to come along and look after them. That meant we had to fork out for our fares on top of our contribution for the in-laws. We'll be scrimping and saving for years to come. Not that I resent the money. Not for Bill. He's a nice old soul. Hen-pecked, but he's always been good to me. But was her ladyship grateful? Was she heck! All she could do was moan. Kept on about the cold and why couldn't we have gone to the Canaries instead. She's always been a misery, but it's as though she was determined to ruin the holiday for everyone else from the moment we stepped on board. The boiled eggs weren't runny enough at breakfast, all the crew are foreigners, the goods in the shops are too expensive, and there are far too many days at sea. She found fault with everything.'

'It can't have been easy for the rest of you.'

'I suppose you heard about that furore in the Atrium Lounge on the morning she died. She was having a right go at the little Filipino waitress for taking so long to bring our order. I tried to calm her down pointing out just how crowded the place was. It was packed to the gills. We were lucky to get a table at all. Doreen ignored me completely and started berating the poor girl again, being downright racially abusive. I told her to stop and that's when she turned on me, calling me a no-good waste of space and how she'd always warned Julie she'd rue the day she married me. It turned into a very public shouting match.' He rubbed his hands over his face. 'She accused me of cheating on Julie. Having an affair with a woman in my office. At the top of her voice, loud enough for the whole ship to hear. Everyone was looking at me as though I was some sort of lowlife. I couldn't take any more. I turned and slunk away with her still screaming after me.'

I put a hand on his shoulder.

'She's been whispering in Julie's ear for weeks now. Then at the beginning of the month, a group from my department went for this conference up in Manchester. When I got back, Doreen accused me of going away for a dirty weekend. I'm pretty sure Julie still half believes it. She went through our joint bank statement pretty carefully when it arrived. I'll swear she was checking I hadn't paid for the hotel room or took out enough cash to cover it. And then to cap it all, a few hours after her tirade at me in the lounge, Doreen drops dead of a heart attack and it's all my fault.'

'Is that what the doctor said? That she'd had a heart attack?'

He must have heard the doubt in my voice because he looked up at me.

'Well not in so many words. But what else could it have been? Actually, they've been pretty cagey about the cause of death. Said we'd have to wait for the inquest which won't be until we get the body back to England.'

'But that's not for another eleven days.'

'Tell me about it! In the meantime, I'm *persona non grata* with the rest of the family and my wife refuses to speak to me. Julie is convinced that our little spat is what caused her heart attack.'

'It's probably just the shock of losing her mother. She'll come round.'

He shook his head. 'I'm not so sure. She's moved out of our cabin. Bill and Doreen had a cabin with twin beds, so Julie's moved in with him.'

'I expect that's more to do with wanting to keep an eye on her father than because of you. The poor man must be in pieces.'

He stared at me, biting the inside of his cheek, his brow

creased as though mulling over what I'd said.

'I suppose so. He's not really in a fit state to be left on his own. I'm not sure he's really taken it all in. We were all in the main restaurant waiting for Doreen to join us for afternoon tea, but she didn't appear. The three of us had been up in the Ocean Lounge listening to the string quartet. Doreen doesn't… didn't… like classical music so she said she'd have a lie down in the cabin and join us for tea when it finished. We assumed she must have fallen asleep, so Julie went to get her. When she got to the cabin, there was an officer waiting. Someone came to fetch Bill and me and we were all taken into one of the offices and told Doreen had been found dead. Bill didn't seem to take it in.

*We all went back to Bill's cabin and Julie made him a cup of tea, but then half an hour later, he asked when Doreen was coming back. The doctor had to come and see him.'*

'Poor man.'

He gave a long sigh. 'It doesn't help being stuck in our rooms all day. I went to the restaurant for dinner last night and I could see all the passengers pointing me out and whispering in little groups. I couldn't take it. I had to leave.'

'In a day or two everyone will have forgotten about it, you'll see.'

He didn't look convinced. 'If only they'd let us fly back home yesterday, but now it's too late. Apparently, only one of the ports we're going to in Greenland has an international airport, but it has no flights leaving the day we're there. We have no choice but to stay on board to the bitter end. I'm already going stir crazy on my own.'

'It will get better, I promise.'

'I'm sorry. I shouldn't be burdening you with all this.'

'Don't be silly. If I can help in any way, let me know.' I picked up my abandoned sudoku sheet and scribbled in the margin and handed it to him. 'Here's my name and cabin number. Any time you want to talk, give me a ring. I can't promise I'll be in when you call but just leave a message and I'll get back to you. Now you've got my name, but I don't know yours.'

He smiled for the first time. 'It's Sam. Sam Rider. Like the singer but spelt with an "i" not a "y".'

# Chapter 7

The red light was flashing on the phone when Graham and I returned to our cabin after lunch.

'Someone's left a message.' He started walking to the table, but I pushed past him to get there first.

'I'll see to it,' I said. 'You get yourself ready for your lecture.'

He raised an eyebrow in surprise, shrugged, then he turned and went to get his suit out of the wardrobe.

It hadn't taken long for Sam to get back to me. It was only a couple of hours since we had last spoken. Had something happened?

I pressed the button but the voice I heard wasn't Sam's.

'This is a message for Mrs Mitchell. Please would you come to the Security Office on the main deck at three-thirty this afternoon. Thank you.' It sounded more like a summons than a request.

I turned to Graham. 'Did you hear that? They want me to go to the Security Office again. What on earth do they want now?'

'You won't know till you go, will you?'

'Don't be so irritating. You know what I mean. I gave them a statement two days ago. It's a pain. Paul's lecture is at half-past three, and as we've never been to Greenland and know nothing about the place, I really wanted to hear the port talk.'

'You'll have to watch the recording when they put it up on the television.'

Graham and I left the cabin together at three-fifteen. He left me when we reached the deck for the theatre, and I continued down the next flight of stairs to my appointment. I knew I was still too early, but there seemed little point in sitting in the cabin twiddling my thumbs. Most of the ship's offices are grouped together alongside the jewellery shop on the starboard side of the ship.

As I tried to waste five minutes wandering around the counters looking at the gaudy displays of diamond necklaces, rings and bracelets and the famous name watches, I couldn't help thinking – misery though she been – Doreen had a point. Nothing came with a price tag of less than three figures. How on earth did such concessions make any money? What might prove profitable for them in the shops amidst the brash glitz-and-glamour style promoted by the American cruise conglomerates might not prove quite so lucrative on this ship. The British-owned Cygnet Cruise Line liked to promote its modest fleet of three vessels in the up-market bracket, but it was far from the priciest in the small ships market. Most of its passengers were retired professionals who were prepared to pay for a degree of luxury but wanted good value for their hard-earned cash. Maybe in the past, holidaymakers might have been more easily lulled into splashing out and spoiling themselves, especially on formal nights when the woman dressed in long evening gowns resplendent in glittering jewellery with their menfolk in dinner-jackets and bow ties. But these days, most of the passengers were seasoned travellers who thought twice about parting with such large sums on impulse even if their purchases came tax-free.

Inevitably, an eager assistant was at my side in seconds.

'I was just looking.' I gave him a weak smile and fled.

There were few people about, but I had no intention of standing outside the door like some naughty schoolgirl waiting to be summoned into the headmaster's study. I did a slow circuit of the deck, passing along the corridor to the rear stairs and lift area, back along the port side though reception and on into the Atrium Lounge.

There was still a minute to go when I knocked on the door.

'Come in.'

The security officer rose from behind his desk and held out his hand for me to shake.

'Mrs Mitchell. Thank you for coming.'

The man seated next to him also got to his feet and unlike the security officer, gave me a warm smile. His grip was firm, but he said nothing. Not even to introduce himself. Though I had only seen him at a distance across the crowded lounge, I recognised him straight away by the three-piece suit he was wearing. Close up, he was quite ordinary and unremarkable looking – early-fifties, receding straw-coloured hair flecked with grey. Were it not for the suit, he would have been unremarkable amongst the ship's casually dressed passengers.

They both sat down again, and I took the chair on the other side of the desk facing them.

The security officer gave a polite smile that failed to reach his eyes, which did nothing to ease my apprehension. 'I wanted to ask you about when you found Mrs Doreen Bowland's body.'

'But I've already given you my statement.'

'True, but it would be helpful if you would give us more detail.'

I had to go through the whole thing again from the moment I left my cabin.

'Were the lift doors open or closed when you arrived.'

'Closed. But they opened straight away so the lift was already on my deck.'

'You are certain she was already dead?'

It proved difficult to give a coherent account of what I'd seen and done because the security officer kept interrupting with questions and backtracking until I was so confused it was difficult to remember the exact sequence of events.

'I shouted for help and when no-one came, I realised that the lift went straight down to the medical centre, so I thought it best to get proper medical help as soon as possible. I do have a first aid certificate, but I've never had to use it in a real situation.'

'And you are certain that you did not move the body at all?'

I was beginning to get annoyed. He'd asked me that several times already. 'Positive.'

'Not even when you put your cheek to her mouth to check if she was breathing?'

'Absolutely certain. I tested her pulse with two fingers on the vein in her neck, so I didn't need to lift her wrist.'

'But you say her body was still warm?'

'Yes.'

He turned to look at the man in the suit who had been silent up to now.

'Just one question, Mrs Mitchell.' The voice was soft and without the hint of accusation that had crept into the security officer's tone. 'Can you remember exactly how the body was lying when the lift doors opened?'

I didn't answer straight away.

'Mrs Mitchell?'

'This is going to sound odd…' He gave me an encouraging smile. 'It didn't really strike me at the time, but when I thought about it later, there was something not quite right about the position she was in.'

'In what way?'

'If someone has a sudden heart attack, I'd expect them to clutch their chest in agony.'

Neither man made any comment.

'Her eyes were open, and her expression was more one of surprise than pain. If she'd had a sudden brain haemorrhage, wouldn't she have just crumpled to the ground or slid down the back wall? She was lying with her legs splayed out towards the door with her bottom eighteen inches from the backwall with just her shoulders against it. When the doctor

47

pulled her body forward to use the defibrillator, it left a long smear of blood down the wall.'

I noticed the man in the suit was busy making notes.

'Then quite obviously, she must have tripped as she went to get out of the lift, fallen backwards and banged the back of her head causing a fatal bleed on the brain,' snapped the security officer. 'A dreadful accident.'

He picked up the papers lying in front of him, tapped the edges together on the desk and placed them in a cardboard file. He snapped the cover closed and looked up at me.

'I think that will be all for now, thank you, Mrs Mitchell.' As I got to my feet, he continued, 'And I am sure I do not need to remind you, as I know the captain told you, it is imperative that you do not discuss this matter with any of the guests.'

'Quite understood.'

I was already at the door, my hand on the handle, when the man in the suit said, 'Just one more question, Mrs Mitchell. Did you hear anyone in the far corridor or when you first reached the landing?'

I turned to face him shaking my head. 'No.'

'You heard no one on the stairs?'

'The whole area seemed deserted.'

He smiled. 'Thank you.'

As I headed for the stairs, I glanced at my watch. There was still time to catch the end of Paul's talk. Rather than trying to sneak into the back of the theatre and disturbing anyone, I decided to return to the cabin and watch it on the television where all the events taking place in the theatre were filmed and shown live on the entertainment channel.

It seemed like a good idea but proved to be more difficult than I imagined. I confess I'm not the most technically-minded individual – I leave all that sort of thing to Graham who is much more adept with any kind of gadgetry than I am. It took more than ten minutes to sort through the various menus until I could find the right channel. By the time I'd arranged the pillows and settled myself back on the bed, the lecture was almost over. Not that I could concentrate anyway. I was far too keyed up.

The most popular seats in the theatre are always towards the back nearest to the entrance doors, so other lecturers and their partners are expected to sit at the front of the auditorium. Not that it was a problem in itself, but it meant that I would have to wait for Graham as he would be one of the last to leave the theatre.

I jumped to my feet the moment the door opened. 'Was it good?'

'Very enjoyable, but how did you get on? Did you find out how the woman died?'

I raised my eyes to the ceiling. 'You're joking. The security officer kept making me go over what happened, over and over again. Firing questions at me as though he was trying to catch me out.'

'He sounds a right jobsworth.'

I snorted. 'You can say that again!'

My sense of outrage suddenly left me and feeling more than a little weepy, I ran towards him. He put his arms around me, and I held him close, my head on his chest.

After a few moments, he said, 'Let's sit down and you can tell me all about it.'

He took my hand and led me to the two easy chairs by the French window.

'He wasn't nearly as bad as that when I went to fill in the incident form a couple of days ago. Perhaps he was trying to impress the other chap?'

'What do you mean?'

'The man who came on board in Reykjavik. He was there.'

'The one the captain came down to meet?'

'I told you at the time I thought he was here about the dead body.'

'So who was he?'

'I've no idea. We weren't introduced.'

'He was the one giving you a grilling, was he?'

I shook my head. 'No. As I said, it was the security officer who treated me like some suspect in a murder enquiry. Mr Brown Suit did ask a couple of questions right at the end, but he was quite pleasant.'

'So, after all that, you didn't learn anything.'

'Only that the security officer now seems determined to pass off her death as an unfortunate accident – banging her head on the wall of the lift when she tripped – but now I'm more convinced than ever there was something suspicious about Doreen Bowland's death.'

Graham frowned and pursed his lips. 'You have absolutely no evidence to suggest that. You're spending far too much time speculating on that woman. I'll be glad when we get to Nuuk, and we can get off the ship. Then you'll have other things to occupy your over-active imagination.'

'Don't worry. I have absolutely no intention of playing detective, I assure you.' I looked at my watch. 'We're too late now for scones and jam, but shall we go and get ourselves a pot of tea?'

# Day 9

*Cruising Prince Christian Sound*

*The scenic sixty-mile-long passage of Prince Christian Sound separates the mainland from Christian IV Island and the other islands that make up the Cape Farewell Archipelago off Greenland's southern tip. It connects the Labrador Sea on the west with the Irminger Sea on the east. The explorer, John Cabot described it as 'a river of melted snow.'*

*Ships can only make the journey through the sound during the summer months, when there is less chance of ice blocking the entrance.*

*Our journey through the narrow channel will provide memorable views of impressive glaciers that cut through its steep mountain sides topped with towering spires and jagged ridges, plus close-up views of icebergs.*

Extract from the Cygnet Daily

# Chapter 8

'Finally, it will take all day for the ship to sail through Prince Christian Sound to reach the Labrador Sea, but if you want to fully appreciate Greenland's most scenic inland passage, do spend some time during the day up on the observation deck. I assure you; it will be worth braving the cold to see the glaciers calving deep valleys into the precipitous mountain sides of the narrow fjord and the beauty of the icebergs that fill the channel. Wrap up well, it will be cold, but I'm reliably informed the crew will be up there with hot chocolate laced with Baileys to keep us all warm. Thank you, ladies and gentlemen, for coming to my lecture and have a wonderful day and enjoy what will be the experience of a lifetime.'

The lights went up and the audience dutifully clapped.

I turned to Graham in the seat next to me. 'After all that, I hope you now know your growlers from your bergy bits and your behemoths?'

He laughed. 'And I expect you to tell me how old they are by the colour of the ice.'

'Our Sybil may not be the most charismatic lecturer on the circuit, but she certainly knows her stuff and those pictures she showed were stunning.'

We stayed sitting in our seats waiting until the crowds had cleared.

The ship was due to arrive at the entrance to the Sound at around 11 o'clock and Dr Adams' lecture – the only one scheduled for the day – had been brought forward half an hour to give everyone the opportunity to be out on deck for what promised to be a spectacular event.

We returned to the cabin to collect extra sweaters, anoraks, woolly hats and gloves.

'What are you giggling at?' Graham asked in mock indignation.

'Not you, darling. Though I have to say, you do look rather fetching with those dangling tassels on the earflaps of your Peruvian hat. It just struck me that it's the first week of August. Everyone back home is sweltering in the hottest temperatures in Britain since records began, and here we are dressed-up like Michelin men.'

'Instead of standing here trading insults, if we want to have a chance of getting anywhere near the rail to see anything, let's get going. Don't forget your binoculars.'

The ship was still some way off the coast but already the crowd was four or five people deep at the prow on the observation deck, but we were able to squeeze through to the rail further back on the starboard side.

'Can you see the channel?' I asked. 'The ship seems to be heading for that large iceberg.'

'Someone said it's sitting in the entrance,' replied the woman standing next to me. 'I hope that doesn't mean it's going to stop us from going in.'

'I don't suppose so. The bridge crew will have a much better picture.'

The woman gave a little shiver. 'Icebergs always make me think of the Titanic.'

'I'm sure our captain knows exactly what he's doing, and I think you'll find ship technology has advanced quite a bit in the last century. Still, I know what you mean, there is something a bit spooky about them the closer you get. All silent and looming.'

It was half an hour later before we were close enough to see that iceberg was not blocking the actual entrance, but the ship slowed right down and gave the floating mountain a wide berth.

'I wish I'd put two pairs of socks on,' I said stamping my feet. 'The rest of me is fine, but my toes are getting frozen. I should have put my boots on rather than trainers.'

'Do you want me to get you a hot chocolate?'

One of the crew arrived carrying a tray of drinks so Graham was spared the journey. Unfortunately, thick ski-type gloves are not the easiest things to grip with. I'm not sure quite what happened, either I squeezed the paper cup too tight, or it slipped between my fingers as I turned back to the rail, but I managed to spill it.

'My gloves are soaked. I'll have to go back to the cabin.'

Graham glanced at his watch. 'It's a bit early for lunch. I was planning on going onto the other side of the ship to take a few more photos.'

'That's fine. I'm getting a bit cold up here anyway. You take as long as you like and when you're ready, come down and get me then we'll go and eat.'

Back in the cabin, I pulled out the dirty washing bag from the back of the wardrobe. I hadn't realised just how full it had become. Probably not a good idea to add wet gloves to the pile anyway. There was a good chance, with most people either outside or watching the scenery from the lounge windows, that one of the washing machines in the laundry would be free. If I dropped off a load on the way up to the Ocean Café, it would probably be finished by the time we'd eaten.

The small icebergs that drifted past the cabin window seemed so much nearer than on the observation deck, so I decided to go out onto the balcony and take a picture. I slipped on my padded jacket and drew back the French window.

It was impossible to take photos wearing gloves but after ten minutes, my bare hands were freezing. Nonetheless, I had managed to get some spectacular shots. Or at least, I hoped they'd prove to be when I looked at them later. One low, oblong-shaped berg with a flat top looked like a table covered in a dark blue cloth. It didn't take much imagination to be able to make out all sorts of creatures in the weathered ice. It was easy to see why Inuit mythology is full of strange sea monsters. Strangely shaped ice remnants appearing out of the mists in the dark winter months, was enough to test the strongest nerve of any lone fisherman adrift in a canoe in a cold sea.

With the balcony door closed to keep in the warm, I didn't hear Graham come into the cabin until the French window slid open.

'They all look so much bigger at this level,' I said. 'Don't you think that one looks just like a bear?'

'Or a huge cat.'

Needless to say, it was another ten minutes before I could persuade him to put down the camera and go for lunch.


When we arrived at the Ocean Café, as was only to be expected, though there was plenty of room inside, all the window tables were taken.

'We could try the other side.'

'I doubt there's any point. There's a couple of seats at that table down the end there. We could see if they'd mind us joining them.'

Sue and Colin were only too happy to have new people to chat to.

'I think that's half the fun of cruising, meeting new people,' Sue assured us. Even though it was only lunchtime and nearly all the passengers were spending the day out on deck bundled up in coats, hats and scarves admiring the scenery, she was in full makeup. Her luminous candyfloss pink lipstick clashed with the glaring red hair which owed more to her hairdresser than to nature.

It wasn't long before she was regaling us with stories about their previous cruises and how much they preferred this ship to others they had been on.

'It seems a lot more friendly than some of the other lines, and we both much prefer smaller ships like this, don't we,

Colin?'

'Oh yes.' Her husband nodded. 'We've been on some of those big ones with two to three thousand passengers and you spend half your time finding your way round the ship.'

'And you never see the same people twice,' she cut in. 'I suppose if you want to spend time on the slot machines or playing roulette and the like in the casinos, those big ships are fine, but that's just not us.'

She was in the middle of telling us about their Reykjavik excursion to the Blue Lagoon when an announcement came over the tannoy.

'Code alpha, code alpha. Stretcher party to Deck 8. Stretcher party to Deck 8.'

'Oh dear. That's the observation deck, isn't it?'

Sue spent the next ten minutes telling us about how on one of their Mediterranean cruises, a woman who had slipped in the shower and broken her hip had to be airlifted off the ship.

'We were all made to vacate the Ocean Lounge and all the forward cabins for when the helicopter came. It's a safety measure, apparently. It was quite exciting really. Our cabin was in the middle of the ship, and we went out on our balcony to watch. The helicopter circled the ship three times, and we could see the paramedic sitting in the open doorway with his legs dangling over the side.'

Colin took out his phone. 'I've got a picture somewhere.'

He must have seen the pained look on Graham's face as he showed us the photo because he quickly snapped off his phone and put it back in his pocket. 'Bit ghoulish really, I suppose,' he muttered, 'but everyone was doing it.'

'We didn't see the poor woman being winched up on a stretcher though,' Sue went blithely on. 'I wonder if the poor person who fell up on Deck 8 will have to be taken off too.'

'Only if it's life-threatening,' her husband said, sagely. 'Besides, where would they take them to? We're in the middle of nowhere. Heaven knowns where the nearest big town with a decent-sized hospital might be.'

The waiter came to collect our empty dessert plates and offered to fetch us tea or coffee.

'I'll pass if you don't mind. I'd like to get back up top and take some more photos,' said Graham, who was already on his feet, pulling on the padded jacket he'd left over the back of the chair.

I stood up to join him.

'You're not stopping for coffee either?' Sue looked quite forlorn at the prospect of loosing her audience.

I shook my head. 'It was nice talking to you. I expect we'll bump into you both again soon.'

'Not if I can help it,' muttered Graham once we were out of earshot. 'Does that woman ever stop talking!'

I suppressed a giggle. 'Don't be such a grouse. We've met worse.'

When we reached the stairs, I said, 'I'm just going down to check on the washing. I'll join you in a bit.'


Graham's woollen shirts and our thick walking socks take a long time to dry. I'd already been to check once that afternoon, but it wasn't until gone four o'clock that I remembered I'd still left things in the tumble-dryer.

The laundry room is on the deck above ours. Passengers rightly get annoyed when people don't empty the machines when they are waiting to use them, I was in a rush as I hurried down the corridor and I failed to notice a door opening. Before I could stop myself, I'd crashed into someone.

'I'm so sorry,' I gasped.

'My fault, I should have looked before I came out.'

Only when we stepped back from each other did I recognise him.

'Sam! How are you?'

He gave a long sigh. 'I've just come back from the infirmary. Julie rang me at lunch time to say Bill had fallen on the steps on the observation deck. The doctor took lots of x-rays and nothing is broken, thank goodness, but he's badly bruised and pretty shaken up. They are not very happy with his heartrate and his stats are very low – whatever that means. He's still hooked up to a machine and they want to keep him down there under observation. Julie persuaded the medical staff to let her stay with him for a while longer.'

'Have you got time for a coffee? I just need to collect my washing and then let's go somewhere quiet and talk.'

# Chapter 9

Graham was none too pleased when I got back to the cabin.

'Where have you been? You said you were only going to collect the washing and were coming straight back to join me on the observation deck. I waited for half an hour then went to look for you. I tried the laundry, the restaurant in case you'd gone for afternoon tea and then I wandered all the way round the Atrium Lounge three or four times.'

'I'm so sorry. I met Sam. He was in bits. He needed someone to talk to, so we went for a coffee at the drinks station in the library.'

It took a while to calm Graham down, but once I'd told him about Bill's fall, he was a bit more sympathetic.

'As though that wasn't bad enough, Sam was summoned to the security office again this morning. They asked him all sorts of questions about the relationship he had with his mother-in-law and then grilled him about the argument he had with her in the lounge. You have to wonder why they are making such a big thing of it. Apparently, Mr Brown Suit was in on the interview just like he was with me.'

'I expect the company is worried that they could be sued by the family for being responsible for her death in some way. Mr Brown Suit is probably someone high up in head office.'

'It's possible, I suppose.'

'If it happened the way the security officer suggested, as the result of a fall, and it was found to be as a consequence of a slippery floor or what-have-you, then the result could prove very expensive if the family decided to sue, and even more disastrous for the company in terms of their reputation – a PR nightmare.'

'Hmm.'

Graham's explanation was perfectly logical, but I couldn't shake the feeling that there was more to Doreen's death than an accident. It might just explain why the security officer was so uptight, but Mr Brown Suit didn't strike me as a head office man. His suit was too off-the-peg and a shade too shabby for a senior, presumably highly paid, official of a major company.

There are usually three to four formal nights on board the ship depending on the length of the cruise. Ladies are expected to wear a cocktail or evening gown and men, a dinner jacket or a dark lounge suit and tie.

'I take it you don't want to go to the pre-dinner captain's cocktail party?' I said, as Graham struggled at the dressing table mirror trying to arrange his bow tie.

The frown he threw in my direction was answer enough.

Standing around in a tightly packed Ocean Lounge making small talk with a group of strangers and trying not to spill a glass of tepid sparkling wine as you attempt to eat squidgy canapes without spilling them down your posh outfit, is no more Graham's idea of fun than it is mine.

There was however, one thing we could not escape. Guest lecturers were expected to host a table at dinner in the main restaurant every formal night. Not that I considered them much of a burden and despite his mutterings, I think Graham rather enjoyed them too. And why wouldn't he? Most passengers tend to be fulsome in their praise of his lectures. He always maintained that seated at the same table, our fellow diners had little choice but to say nice things if only to be polite, but secretly he lapped up the acclaim. It may be true that as his wife, I freely admit that I am somewhat prejudiced, but in my opinion, he is one of the best. Plus of course, I love history.

Few of his audience could appreciate the sheer amount of work that went into every single presentation – not just the research but finding suitable illustrations and the hours of work designing and animating the slides. He spends the last week before the cruise practising and polishing until he can speak without having to refer to his notes.

The restaurant was virtually empty by the time we arrived and in no time at all we were being escorted to our table. The smartly dressed Filipino waiter pulled out my chair then deftly unfolded the linen napkin and laid it across my lap the moment I sat down. Graham took the seat opposite me leaving room for two other couples to join us.

'Not many people have arrived yet,' I said, as I glanced around the room.

The Rev. Parker-Scott was sitting at the next table reading his menu. His was also a table for six, but as he was unaccompanied, he would be hosting solo passengers. Cygnet ships had a higher proportion of single cabins than any other cruise line and there were several events organised for single passengers to meet and socialise together should they wish.

Graham and I were soon joined by an older couple from Godalming in the south of the country. Shirley, who with her chestnut hair and artful makeup looked much younger than her years, lost no time in asking Graham about the Vikings and their voyages of discovery which had been the subject of his last lecture. Edgar, who sat next to me, proved to be a pleasant dinner companion with a quick wit which soon had me laughing.

The four of us had been chatting for five minutes or so and were still waiting for another couple to join us when I noticed Graham's eyebrows suddenly shoot skywards. I turn to see what had caught his attention.

A woman was standing in the doorway. The red dress hugged her voluptuous figure like an Argentinian tango dancer. She slowly scanned the room and a slow smile spread over her expertly made-up features when her eyes homed in on the handsome chaplain. She whispered something to the waiter at her side. As she slowly sashayed in our direction, a magnificent diamond pendant nestled in her generous cleavage caught the light. She could not have made a more dramatic entrance with a red rose clenched between her teeth!

The waiter led her to the singles table. The Rev. Parker-Scott rose to his feet, but the closed look on his face suggested he was far from comfortable with the prospect of an evening spent in the company of Cygnet's answer to Mae West.

'I see our merry widow has arrived,' said Shirley, with a deep chuckle. 'And I think our Mona may have set her sights on our good chaplain.'

'I take it you have come across her already?' I asked.

'Oh yes. We were on the same tour in Reykjavik. She sat next to us at lunch in the restaurant,' explained her husband.

'She made no secret of the fact that she's looking for husband number three. Apparently, she met her last one on a cruise ship. The best place to get to know all about someone in a relatively short space of time according to her. She's actually quite a fun person. Had us in stitches most of the time.'

At that point we were joined by another couple and after brief introductions, there was a lull in the conversation as we all studied the menu and made our choices.

The place was almost empty, and the waiters were laying up all the tables around us for breakfast by the time we left.

'That wasn't so bad now, was it?' I said, when we got back to the cabin. 'Admit it, despite all your reservations, that was a very pleasant evening.'

'True.' He gave a grin and wrinkled his nose. 'We were lucky. Shirley and Edgar were a lovely couple. The other pair weren't quite so outgoing, but it was a good evening all round. That first formal evening was dire by comparison, if you remember. That couple from Penzance were hard work, and the other two said barely a word between them.'

'They weren't that bad, though I'll grant you it was a relief when they said they wanted to see the show in the theatre, and we broke up early. So, what do you want to do now?' I glanced at my watch. 'The show in the theatre will be almost over.'

Graham picked up the day's events sheet. 'We haven't missed much. It was a tribute to Sinatra. There's a trivia quiz in the Ocean Lounge followed by dancing to the ship's band or we could go for a drink in one of the bars.'

'How about we stay in the cabin and watch a film?'

'Good idea.' He picked up the television controls. 'What do you fancy? A latest release, action and adventure, drama or comedy.'

'Definitely something light. How about a comedy?'

# Day 10

## At Sea

*Tomorrow we will arrive in Greenland, the world's largest island which covers an area of over 836,000 square miles. Nevertheless, with a population of just over 56,000, it is the least densely populated area in the world.*

*Although geologically it is part of the Canadian Shield made up of Precambrian rock that dates back four billion years, historically its links have always been with Europe.*

*Today the ice sheet is melting at an alarming rate. If its mile-thick ice sheets were to melt, sea level would rise twenty-three feet.*

*Erik the Red was described in medieval and Icelandic sagas as having founded the first settlement in Greenland. In 982, Erik was banished from Iceland for three years. He sailed west and eventually reached the coast of Greenland. When he returned to Iceland, he tried to persuade others to help establish a colony on the island. He gave it the name Greenland because he believed "men will desire much the more to go there if the land has a good name".*

*He sailed with twenty-five ships and more than four hundred people but only fourteen ships arrived safely. The others were either lost at sea or returned to Iceland because of the bad weather.*

*The Vikings established two major colonies. The first was the Eastern settlement which is the area where we will be visiting after Nuuk. Erik the Red built his farm not far from present-day Qaqortoq. Another group established the Western settlement further up the coast around Nuuk.*

*From about 1000 AD, Inuit peoples also arrived but there was little interaction between the two communities.*

*The Viking colony that Erik the Red established survived for around five hundred years and grew to around five thousand people at its peak. But in a relatively short space of time, the colony died out. The most likely explanation appears to be a combination of factors including overgrazing and climate change. Sea ice increased, which meant the seals and the whales failed to return, and ocean storms made putting out to sea even more hazardous.*

*By the time the eighteenth century Danish-Norwegian Lutheran missionary Hans Egede arrived to convert them to the true faith, there was no sign of the first Viking settlers.*

*Denmark took control of all trade and Greenland remains part of the Kingdom of Denmark. Home rule was established in 1979.*

Extract from the Cygnet Daily

# Chapter 10

Graham's morning lecture had been well received but after lunch he complained of feeling tired and decided to take a nap. The book I was reading proved to be too slow-moving with too many characters to hold my attention so, feeling somewhat aimless, I took a stroll around the ship.

I spotted Mr Brown Suit on one of the decks overlooking the atrium. He'd abandoned the suit jacket and striped, green tie and was sitting back in an easy chair, busy writing on the pad balanced on his knee. On the deck below, the young Ukrainian classical pianist playing in the Atrium Lounge came to the end of a Chopin waltz. He put down his pen and clapped. The young woman glanced up at him with a smile and a nod of acknowledgement.

'I often think being one of the resident musicians must be one of the worst jobs on the ship,' I said as I passed by and caught his eye.

He raised an eyebrow. 'How so?'

'She's obviously highly trained and very talented as most of them are, but to have to perform what is essentially background music week after week must be quite galling. Most people down there are either having tea or simply socialising. I doubt that many are actually there to hear her play. A few may give perfunctory applause now and again but not many.'

'True. But then I don't suppose there are a great many opportunities for young musicians these days, and on the plus side, they get free board and lodging whilst they are here, and they get to see the world.'

'That's a very down-to-earth view. Practical, I suppose, but it must be disheartening.' Now I'd softened the ice between us, I decided to ask the question that had been on my mind for several days. 'Would you happen to know if the handbag belonging to the woman who died has turned up, by any chance?'

He gave me a long look before he answered. 'I believe it has.'

'That's good.' Keeping my eyes locked on his, I continued. 'And are you going to tell me where it turned up?'

'Why are you so interested?'

Instead of answering his question, I said, 'Was it mislaid or stolen as she claimed?'

I wasn't sure at first if he would say any more but then he smiled and gestured for me to sit in the chair opposite him.

'It was discovered under one of the serving stands in the restaurant on Sunday morning.'

'But she was sitting in the centre nowhere near a stand.'

'It might have been accidently kicked there.'

I gave a snort. 'You don't believe that any more than I do.'

'Don't I?'

'The important question is, was anything taken?' The man was getting under my skin, and he knew it. 'But I don't suppose for a moment that you'd tell me even if it was.'

'On the contrary, Mrs Mitchell, I am quite happy to tell you. It transpires that Mrs Bowland never carried money or anything of value in her bag while on board, and as far as her family are concerned nothing appears to be missing.'

'How odd.'

'Now I have a question, Mrs Mitchell…'

'Amanda, please.'

'Amanda, why are you so fascinated by the disappearance of Mrs Bowland's bag?'

I gave a long sigh. 'There is something about that poor woman's death that keeps playing on my mind.'

'I don't suppose coming across a dead body is something

that anyone could easily forget about in a hurry.'

'It's not that. I can't help feeling that there was something out of kilter about the way she was lying. It wasn't… natural.'

'In what way?' The gentle, half-mocking attitude he'd had before was now gone. He leant forward, eager for an answer.

'I can picture the scene in my mind, but I just can't work out what doesn't quite add up about it.'

'Close your eyes.'

I stared at him.

'Trust me. Sit back in the chair and relax, then close your eyes.'

I did as he asked and tried to visualise the body.

'The position is all wrong. The shoulders are too high.'

'Couldn't that be the result of her body sliding slowly down the wall?'

'Possibly. But…'

There was a long silence.

*It was as though someone had put their hands under her arms and dragged her into the lift.* There was no way I was going to say those words out loud.

I opened my eyes to see him staring at me intently, but it was impossible to read his expression. But in my own mind, I was now certain that Doreen Bowland had been murdered. If only I knew more about the exact cause of death.

'I don't suppose it's important anyway,' I said quickly, edging my bottom to the front of the chair ready to make my getaway.

'Why do you say that?'

'Well, if she died of natural causes, or as the security officer suggested because she tripped…' I let the sentence hang.

He seemed to read my mind because he gave a deep-throated chuckle and said, 'Nice try, Amanda. But if it is any consolation, until the formal post-mortem can be carried out back in England, nothing can be confirmed.'

'But you must have some idea,' I protested.

He wagged a finger at me.

I pulled a face and made to get up.

'Let me get you a drink before you go.'

'At this time of day?'

'A coffee then.'

I shook my head and stood up. 'I need to go and find my husband but thank you.'

'If you remember anything else, no matter how small a detail that strikes you, do let me know.

'Will do Mr... I don't even know your name. I won't know who to ask for.'

'Jarret. Richard Jarret.'

'But it's not mister is it, Inspector?'

His right eyebrow twitched momentarily, but he made no reply.

I turned and headed back towards the rear stairs unable to suppress a triumphant smile.

# Chapter 11

'But the two things have to be connected,' I protested.

'I can't see how. What possible link could there be between the woman's missing handbag and her death?'

'*Stolen* handbag.'

'You don't know that for a fact.'

'Come on, Graham! Doreen Bowland was nowhere near a serving stand at dinner that evening and more importantly, why did it take three whole days to find it? Like everywhere else on this ship, that restaurant is thoroughly cleaned from top to bottom every single day.'

He shrugged his shoulders. 'Maybe, but I still don't understand why you keep insisting there was something suspicious about her death.'

'Bringing a detective on board confirms it.'

'There you go again. You don't *know* Mr Brown Suit is a policeman. You're jumping to conclusions. And even if he is, it might just be protocol in the case of an unexplained death. It could just be the cruise line covering all bases. It doesn't mean it's suspicious let alone that she was murdered.'

'But the position of the body…'

'Could be explained by her legs slipping from under her as she fell back sliding down the wall just as this Jarret fellow suggested.'

'But…' It was pointless trying to make him understand. He hadn't seen what I'd seen or talked with Richard Jarret. Admitting defeat, I put on my best smile and said as brightly as I could manage, 'Teatime. It must be almost four o'clock.'

He smiled back. 'Good idea. Let me just put some shoes on.'


Paul and Margaret were in the corridor when we went out.

'I didn't realise you were in the room next to us,' said Margaret. 'Are you going to the afternoon tea as well?'

'We were heading down to the Atrium Lounge for a cup of tea,' I said tentatively.

'But they're doing a special chocolate tea party in the restaurant this afternoon. You must come and join us.'

She sounded so pleased at the prospect that I didn't like to disappoint her. Mustering a smile, I said, 'Sounds a lovely idea. After you.'

The restaurant was filling up fast by the time we arrived, and we were ushered to a table not far from the buffet in the centre of the room. I quickly took the chair facing away from all the tempting cakes.

'I made a firm resolution before I came on board that I would not go home any heavier than when I came,' I said to Margaret as we sat down. 'You do realise that you persuading me to come for a chocolate tea is putting all those good intentions into jeopardy, don't you. It's alright for you. You're as slim as a fashion model.'

She gave a tinkling laugh. 'You have to spoil yourself occasionally. And it's such a shame not to enjoy all the lovely food on offer. Besides, you can always make up for it by using the stairs and not the lifts when you go up for dinner tonight.'

'I do that every day,' I wailed.

The next half hour passed pleasantly enough. Paul did most of the talking. Though this would be the first time that any of us had been to Greenland, Paul and Margaret had travelled extensively.

'We were in the West Indies in January and around South America in the spring, so this end of the Atlantic is a bit of a change,' Paul said smugly.

'That sounds exciting. Have you been doing this sort of thing for long?'

'It must be ten years now. I'm lucky being self-employed. Means I can fit things round any cruising opportunities I might fancy.'

'So, what line of work are you in?'

'Finance.'

The curt answer made me feel that I'd asked an impertinent question. I confess I wouldn't recognise a Rolex unless I was close enough to read the label, but the gold wristwatch he was sporting looked very expensive and Margaret had more rings on her fingers than I have in my jewellery box. Whatever Paul did for a living, he was clearly very successful.

Paul turned to Graham. 'So are Vikings your area of speciality?'

'Not really. I've had to do quite a bit of work for this trip. Most of my lectures are concerned with Ancient Rome and Greece so most of our cruises up to now have been in the East Mediterranean.'

Margaret and I went to inspect the selection of cakes on offer leaving the two men to talk shop. At the central buffet, we waited for the grossly over-weight man in front of us to finish. He was trying to balance a large slice of chocolate gateau on top of a plate already laden with several chocolate scones, a large dollop of clotted cream plus various other chocolate concoctions.

Margaret glanced at me and raised her eyes heavenwards. When he was out of earshot, she whispered. 'Heart attack waiting to happen.'

She helped herself to a chocolate macaroon and two small squares of what looked like flapjack covered in chocolate. Feeling quite virtuous, I picked up two fruit skewers consisting of strawberries, banana slices and chunks of apple then spoilt it all by holding them in the chocolate fountain.

'I can't believe the amount of food some people put away

when they come on a cruise,' said Margaret when we got back to the table. 'Have you noticed at breakfast how many people help themselves to the full works? Egg, bacon, sausage, tomatoes, mushrooms, baked beans and fried bread and when they've polished off all that, they go back for Danish pastries and croissants. They can't possibly eat that much at home.'

'Perhaps they're building up their reserves ready to hibernate until the next cruise,' joked Paul.

'Talking of heart attacks, I haven't seen that dead woman's family around the ship for the last few days.' Margaret glanced round the room. 'I assume they flew back home when we were in Reykjavik.'

'No. They are still here. I saw her son-in-law yesterday,' I told her.

'Really!' Margaret sounded surprised. 'That must be very difficult for them.'

Paul gave a snort. We all looked at him. 'I should think it must be easier for them without her upsetting everyone she came in contact with the whole time.'

Graham asked, 'What did she do to upset you?'

'She buttonholed me outside the theatre and proceeded to complain about the tour she went on in Kirkwall. I tried to point out politely that I don't have anything to do with the tours themselves and that I'm here only to tell passengers about what is on offer. She then told me that I should have pointed out exactly how much walking was involved and how many steps.'

'It was very embarrassing,' Margaret broke in. 'She was holding up all the people trying to leave the theatre and shouting at the top of her voice.

'I wouldn't mind, but I'd done exactly that. I'm always careful to tell people exactly what is involved, and which excursions aren't suitable for people with walkers, but there was no reasoning with her.'

'She even demanded that Paul reimburse the cost of the excursion. Not just for her but her whole family.'

'Eventually, her daughter managed to pull her away, but she was still shouting after me as Margaret and I beat a hasty retreat. The next morning, Liam the tours manager, told me the objectional woman had made an official complaint. Not that anything came of it. The woman was dead the day after. But it still doesn't put me in a good light with the company and you never know what effect that has on the reviews you get from other passengers at the end of the cruise.'

'It's not worth worrying about,' I told him. Time to change the subject. 'Talking of excursions, have you been asked to do any escorting in Nuuk tomorrow?'

'I said I was happy to play Tail-end Charlie on the hike and Margaret's doing the visit to a local family. What about you two?'

'We both put down for something, but I've no idea which ones.' Graham looked at me. 'Do you remember, love?'

'I know I opted for the walking tour of the town, and I think there's a boat trip safari in the fjord that you said you fancied. Though I seem to recall you saying something about expecting that quite a few of the crew might be interested in escorting that trip, so chances were that you'd get put on something else.'

'That rings a bell. We'll just have to wait and see what they have lined up for us when we go down to collect our rucksacks.'

By then, the restaurant was almost deserted, and the staff were beginning to clear the tables.

'I think they're waiting to lay up for dinner tonight,' I said. 'Time to go, folks.'

It was probably Margaret's earlier comments that made me think about Doreen Bowland's death as I stood in front of the mirror putting on my makeup before dinner. Not that the picture of her collapsed corpse hunched in the corner of the lift was ever far from my mind. Her death nagged at me like a dull toothache.

'Penny for them.' Graham's voice broke my reverie.

'Just thinking.'

'Obviously. What's so engrossing that it's kept you standing there poised with that lipstick in your hand for so long? It's that dead woman again, isn't it?'

I gave a long sigh. 'I can't get her out of my mind. I may not have any real medical training, but only a full autopsy report would convince me that her demise was due to some clinical cause.'

I turned to look at him. He put his hands on his hips.

'Before you say anything, the position of her body wasn't consistent with an accident. I'm convinced she was hoisted under the armpits and dragged to the back of the lift. And that leaves only one other possibility.'

He drew in a deep breath. I rushed on, 'I know, I know. You have every reason to be sceptical. But I've been thinking. When I was on the excursion in Isafjordur, I talked with a lovely old dear who told me that she left her cabin at three o'clock in the morning to get a mug of hot chocolate. When she tried to go down in the lift, she was told to use the other set at the other end of the ship because they were cleaning the carpet. Something was obviously going on because there were no lights in the stairwell. How can you shampoo carpets in the dark? The only reason to switch off the light is because they were testing for blood. Luminol spray can only be detected by a blue light in the dark.'

'Even if your wild theory could possibly be the case, aren't you forgetting something? Who would want to murder her? Granted, the woman was objectionable in capital letters and had gone out of her way to upset almost everyone with whom she came in contact, but that's hardly grounds to kill her. She'd only been on the ship for three days, surrounded by strangers apart from her family.'

'I appreciate that, and for the life of me, I can't come up with a motive. The person who took the brunt of her venom was Sam, but although I've only talked to him a couple of times, I find it impossible to picture her son-in-law as a killer.'

'Isn't that reason enough to leave it to the police?'

'You said earlier you didn't believe Richard Jarret was a detective.'

Graham threw his hands up in the air. 'Amanda Mitchell, you are the most stubborn, frustrating woman I have ever met. For heaven's sake, finish your makeup and let's get to dinner before they close the Ocean Café.'

# Day 11

*Nuuk, Greenland*

*Lying on the southwest coast, Nuuk is the capital of the autonomous island of Greenland. It lies roughly on the same latitude as Reykjavik and is home to a third of the country's population. It is surrounded by water and impressive mountains and there are no major roads out of the city to link it with other towns. The only way to get around is by sailing or flying.*

*The city was founded by the Norwegian-Dutch missionary Hans Egede. Egede had seen it as his mission to bring the reformed Lutheran church to the early Viking settlers. Though the Norse people had long died out by the time he arrived, he remained in Greenland to convert the Inuit. Given that today ninety-five percent of Greenlanders identify as Christian, he obviously did a good job.*

*Egede established a mission house on an island just offshore from present day Nuuk. A small town developed and it became a trading post. It began to grow as a fishing harbour and the port is still home to almost half of Greenland's fishing fleet. The contribution of the fishing industry has declined in importance in Nuuk as the town's economy has developed rapidly since the 1970s and 1980s.*

*The population has doubled since Greenland was granted home rule from Denmark. Attracted by good employment opportunities with high wages, Danes have continued to settle in the town. Today, Nuuk has the highest proportion of Danes of any town in Greenland. Half of Greenland's immigrants live in Nuuk, which also accounts for a quarter of the country's native population.*

*Nuuk is home to Greenland's only university built in 1995. Many students still need to travel to Denmark for their higher education in certain subjects.*

Extract from the Cygnet Daily

# Chapter 12

It was a leisurely start to the day the next morning. My walking tour wasn't until ten o'clock and although Graham had been asked to escort the boat safari, his was the afternoon excursion rather than the morning one.

'It means we're not going to spend much of the day together,' Graham said as we climbed up to the top deck for breakfast.

'When do we ever?' I laughed.

'True, but today you'll just about be getting back to the ship as I leave.' He looked quite forlorn.

'I think you'll cope without me. You should be back soon after four o'clock so, if you've worked up an appetite after climbing up Mount Quassussuaq, we could go for afternoon tea together.'

Our guide was waiting for us by the coach when we all got off the ship. She was a short, round-faced Inuit woman and full of fun. Once we were all seated, she introduced herself as Tatkret which apparently meant moon, which is what she said we could call her.

It was only a ten-minute coach ride from the port to the centre of the modern town where our walking tour would begin. I knew from Paul's port talk that it was the world's northernmost capital and also one of the smallest in terms of its population, but then the whole country had fewer people than our own hometown of Oxford back in England.

On the journey, Moon told us something of the town's history which dated back to the early eighteenth century. The journey was so short that I hadn't bothered to get out my little notebook. I've never kept a diary, but when we first started going abroad, I did keep a holiday journal. Once Graham became a cruise ship speaker, there never seemed time to write it up every evening but I still take a small notebook in my pocket to jot down anything special I see or the odd snippet of information.

Everyone trooped off the coach and Moon led our party along the modern high street towards the older part of town. Much to my relief, there was no one with any walking difficulties amongst the twenty or so passengers. With any luck, that would make my job of keeping an eye on any stragglers a whole lot easier.

Our first stop was at a large modern bronze statue in front of the parliament house.

'This is Kaassassuk, the boy who never grew up. The legend goes that he lost his parents when he was only a baby and was brought up by the villagers. But they treated him badly because he was so small. Do you see his big nostrils? That's because all the bigger boys would stick two fingers up his nose and lift him up and swing him around. So, one day he ran away into the wilderness to search for the Lord of Power. When the Lord of Power appeared, Kaassassuk told him how he wanted to be big and strong like the other boys. The monster picked him up by the leg and shook him until all his toys fell out of his pockets. He told him that from then on, he would have great strength. Kaassassuk returned to the village, but he concealed these new powers until one day three polar bears threatened the village, and he killed them all. Frightened that he might turn on them for treating him so badly in the past, the people tried to curry favour with Kaassassuk, but in vain. He took a terrible revenge, squeezing them all to death. So, the moral of the legend is to treat everyone with kindness and respect.'

Most people had taken their photos by the time Moon had

finished her story and as the party moved on, there were only a couple of stragglers still snapping away that I had to wait for. The man hurried to join his wife before the group had gone fifty yards or so, but the other person seemed set on taking the statue from every angle.

'Sorry to hold you up, flower.' She gave me a broad grin.

'No problem. You're travelling on your own, I take it?'

'That's me. Would you mind holding this while I put my gloves back on? My fingers are freezing, but it's impossible to take photos with gloves on.' She thrust her camera into my hands.

'Thanks. I'm Mona by the way. Mona by name but not by nature.' She gave a hearty laugh.

'Hi. My name's Amanda. I take it you're enjoying the cruise?'

'Very much. What's not to like? Fantastic ship, great food, wonderful staff who can't do enough for you, and friendly company. So, what do you do on the ship?'

'I don't. I'm just a passenger.'

'I thought because you're wearing a red anorak with Cygnet Excursions printed on the back, you were crew.'

I shook my head. 'We get loaned the jackets when we escort one of the tours. The company likes to have an escort on every tour to help look after the group. There are a lot of tours every port day, so the lecturers and their partners are asked to help out. My husband gives the history presentations.'

'I see. Apart from the port talks when I can't make up my mind about which tour to go on, I'm afraid I don't normally bother with the lectures. History's not really my thing. They are usually on at the same time as the craft classes anyway, and I really enjoy those.'

'I've seen some of the lovely things that people have made and I've always fancied trying a craft class, but I feel duty bound to go to the lectures. The other day when I was having coffee in the library, I saw two women finishing off a pretty poppy brooch. The red petals were edged with what

I thought were tiny little beads until they showed me. The beads were actually the teeth from one side of a zip pulled into petal shapes with tiny stitches gathered together on the other edge.'

'That's been my favourite session so far. Sylvia, our teacher, is really good. She's the best craft instructor I've ever had on a cruise.'

Mona chatted away merrily as we caught up with the others who were already making their way inside the National Museum which was housed in a hundred-year-old warehouse.

It was only when Mona pulled off her woolly hat and shook out the blonde waves that fell just below her shoulders that I recognized her. It was hard to equate this wonderfully happy-go-lucky woman with the vamp in the scarlet dress I'd noticed at the formal evening.

The museum's most famous exhibit was a collection of 500-year-old mummies found frozen under a pile of stones in a cave in the far north of the country. The six women and two children were remarkably preserved because of the cold.

'The baby looks like a doll,' whispered Mona. 'The skin looks perfect, not dried up at all like all the other bodies. You can even see its black hair under the hood of his little fur jacket.'

'It is amazing, but I think we're going to get left behind if we're not careful. Everyone else is in the next room.'

Mona didn't seem eager to follow. 'You said you were married to one of the lecturers.'

'That's right. I'm Graham's wife.'

'But you know all the guest speakers?'

'There are different speakers on every cruise, but I've met the others yes.'

'Including Tony?'

I must have looked confused because she added, 'The chaplain.'

'We shook hands at a meeting when we first came on

board, but we've never had a proper conversation.'

'That's a shame. I was hoping you could tell me a bit more about him.'

'I saw you sitting next to him at dinner on the formal night. The two of you seemed to be getting on like a house on fire.'

Her blue eyes sparkled, and her smile lit up her round face, creating attractive dimples in her cheeks. 'Oh yes. He's quite a character and we have so much in common, though I'll admit, it came as a big surprise on the formal night to discover that he was a clergyman.'

'Had you met him before then?'

'We met up in the late-night bar at the start of the cruise. He's a great dancer, knows all the latest club dances and is such fun to be with. You should have seen the pair of us on the dance floor kicking our heels until the early hours.'

'Really?'

'Oh yes. We seemed to really hit it off. He was up there again the next night for the karaoke. I went up and sang one of my old numbers then I persuaded him to have a go. Mind you, we were both more than a little bit tiddly by that stage. He's got a great voice. Everyone demanded an encore. When he asked for requests, I shouted out *Pretty Woman*. I suppose you're too young to remember it. It was one of Roy Orbison's early songs.'

'The one with the sexy growl?'

'That's the one!' She pulled a face. 'You could've knocked me down with a feather when I saw him in his dog collar. That was the last thing I expected. But then I suppose he had to mind his Ps and Qs in front of everyone else at the table.'

'I hope that didn't cramp your style,' I teased.

She gave a wicked laugh and nudged me with her elbow. 'Nothing's going to do that. Life's too short. Live it to the full, that's my motto.'

'Good on ya! So, do the two of you have any more get-togethers planned?'

She tapped the side of her nose. 'Wait and see.'

'Oh! At this rate you'll have him down the aisle before you know it.'

She burst out in raucous laughter and everyone in the room turned to look. She shook her head, linked her arm through mine and made for the door. 'Hardly, flower. I'm not a cougar – he's a good twenty years younger than me, if not more. Besides, can you see me as a vicar's wife?'

# Chapter 13

'Do you mind if we join you?'

'Please do. I've almost finished my lunch anyway, so you can have the table to yourselves,' I said.

'Don't let us drive you away. You were on the same walking tour as us this morning. I thought I recognized you. You were our escort.'

'Oh yes.' I tried to smile encouragingly but, in all honesty, I couldn't place either the plump, middle-aged woman with shoulder-length auburn hair or her balding husband. Not that it was that surprising as we'd all been bundled in padded jackets, woolly hats and scarves plus sunglasses.

'Our guide was excellent, wasn't she? Quite an extrovert. Did you see her climbing on to the ropes in the playground to show us how the children learnt how to roll their canoes when they go out into the fjord?'

We chatted for some time, and I was surprised when I looked at my watch as I left the Ocean Café and realised that I'd been up there for over an hour. Not that it was a problem as there was nothing else I'd been planning on doing until Graham returned. As I walked down the stairs, I tried to make up my mind whether to get changed and go down to the sauna or find a quiet spot somewhere and read. Still deep in thought, I turned onto the corridor not paying much attention to the gaggle of people at the far end.

As I got nearer, I realised it was some of the lecturers and their partners who were talking animatedly outside Sybil's cabin.

As I approached, I could make out Margaret's high-pitched voice.

'But why on earth would anyone want to do anything like that?'

'Do what?' I asked.

'One of the cabins on the deck above has been broken into.' I'd never seen Margaret quite so animated.

'Genevieve saw the captain going in to inspect the damage and now it's all boarded up.'

'The door wasn't damaged,' said the petite, attractive woman with a ready smile who was holding a large pile of laundry. I vaguely recognized her as Sybil's younger sister from the speakers' get-together.

Sybil unlocked the door with her keycard. 'Here, let me take those while you tell Amanda the whole story. I'll put them in our cabin.' She leant back against the open door, put out her arms for the folded washing, then disappeared inside with it.

'Thanks.' Genevieve turned back to me. 'I went up to put some stuff in the washing machine on the next deck up a couple of hours ago. There were a couple of senior officers in the corridor talking to some other people inside one of the cabins just before the laundry. They stepped inside to let me pass. I tried to take a sneaky look inside, but I couldn't see much, what with them in the way, but I could hear a woman's voice. She seemed quite upset.'

'Did you hear what they were saying?'

'Only snatches, but I got the impression the room had been ransacked. Whatever had happened in there must have been quite serious because as I came out of the laundry a few minutes later, I saw the captain and another man just going into the room.'

'So, who was the other man?' I asked.

'No idea.'

'Perhaps it was the woman's husband and that was his cabin,' suggested David.

Genevieve didn't look convinced.

'Have you seen him around the ship before?' I had a sneaking suspicion who it might be.

'I don't think so, but he looked official somehow.'

'In what way?'

'Well for a start, he was wearing a suit. When I went back up before lunch to put everything in the dryer, there were still people in the room and there was one of those small temporary stands in the doorway with "crew only" written on it.'

'I wonder what they were doing,' said Gwen.

'Perhaps they were checking for fingerprints,' suggested Margaret.

'Now you're letting your imagination run away with you, sweetie. I doubt very much they have the equipment, never mind the know-how to be able to do that,' said Paul putting a hand on her shoulder.

'Okay, clever clogs.' Margaret glared up at him, her lips pinched tight. 'What were they doing then?'

He shrugged his shoulders. 'No idea. Perhaps if the place was broken into, they were tidying up the mess. Anyway, if you still want to have a look round the shops, I think we'd better get going or it will be time for the last shuttle bus back to the ship before we even get to the town.'

It was almost half past four before Graham came back to the cabin.

'Hi there. How did it go?'

'Very enjoyable,' he said dropping his rucksack and camera on the bed and peeling off his jacket before disappearing into the bathroom.

'No problems then?' I asked when he emerged again.

'There were only a dozen people on the tour, and they were all regular walkers. Only one woman didn't have proper walking boots, but she was wearing trainers with good thick soles, so it wasn't a problem.'

'Did you get any decent photos?'

'I hope so. I'll be able to tell once I've download them

onto the laptop tonight. How was your trip?'

'Good. Great guide. She told us a couple of Inuit legends I thought you might find useful for one of your lectures if we ever come back here again. I made a few notes for you.'

'Great.'

I hadn't planned to tell him straight away, but as he took his time getting changed and sorting out his gear, I found myself telling him about the shenanigans outside the laundry.

'Now the door is crisscrossed with thick yellow "staff only" sticky tape to stop anyone going in.'

He raised an eyebrow. 'So, you went to look?'

'No,' I said, indignantly, though I'll admit I had thought of doing so. 'Genevieve told us she saw it when she went to collect the washing. The thing is, I've a pretty good idea of whose cabin it might be. I told you I bumped into Sam coming out of his room when I went to collect the washing the other day. From what Genevieve was saying, I think there's a good chance that the one that was ransacked was next to his so it's odds on that it belonged to Doreen and Bill.'

Graham frowned, far from convinced.

Before he could start telling me that I was jumping to conclusions, I rushed on, 'If whoever took Doreen's bag didn't find what he was looking for, it makes sense that he would search her room. The two things have to be connected.'

'Not necessarily.'

'Interesting that Richard Jarret turned up with the captain to see the damage though, wouldn't you say?'

'Not if he is from head office. It's no use looking at me like that. You're just trying to make the facts fit what you yourself admit is a feeling that something wasn't right about that woman's death. You're just not willing to accept there might be a simple explanation – a heart attack, a sudden embolism or as the security officer suggested some sort of accident.'

'But what about the handbag and the room being searched? They can't be a coincidence.'

'You don't even know for sure that it was her cabin that was broken into. It could be anyone's. Perhaps someone didn't close their door properly when they left the cabin. It's easily done. You did the other day when you were in a hurry. Anyone walking down the corridor later might just take their chance and take a quick look round for something they could pocket.'

'Then why leave the place in a mess and alert the owner to the fact that it had been burgled?'

He shrugged his shoulders and changed the subject.

# Chapter 14

After Graham had tucked into a couple of scones plus several finger sandwiches at teatime, it was later than usual when we went up for dinner by which time the Ocean Café had become quite crowded. Not that we were worried about sharing a table. The waiter led us almost to the far end of the room, and I was delighted to see Mona already sitting there.

'Hello again. I don't think you've met my husband Graham, have you?'

'No.' Mona gave him a beaming smile. 'But I've heard all about you and your wonderful history lectures, and not just from Amanda.'

Once we'd all ordered, Mona asked, 'Did you see the production show last night?'

Graham nodded. 'The tribute to *Cabaret*. It was excellent. The show cast are very slick.'

'The costumes were glorious. All those feather boas and frilly skirts. How the dancers manage all those quick changes, I've no idea,' I added.

'Lots of practice,' Mona said, sagely. 'How about the singing? What did you think of that?'

'The fair-haired girl could do with a stronger voice. She was drowned out by the band in some of those numbers, but the one who sang *Don't tell mama*, was superb. It brought the house down. I think that was my favourite song. It's been running through my head all day,' I said.

'She's a natural. Good sense of theatre. She should go far,' Mona agreed. 'Pity about the gold nail varnish.'

'I didn't notice.'

'My choreographer always used to insist on only pink or red. Anything else is unprofessional according to him.'

'I didn't realise you were a dancer, Mona.'

She gave a burble of laughter. 'A singer actually. Of course, it's fifty years ago now, but I did make it to *The Talk of the Town*. Of course, it's long gone now – revamped as a cinema the *Hippodrome*. I had a two-year contract as one of the review singers. Even had my own solo on several occasions. It was the highlight of my stage career. Back then, it was the top venue. The only London nightclub to bring in the big star names like Ertha Kitt, Tony Bennett, Shirley Bassey, Lena Horne and Diana Ross. I even met Diana Dors, wonderful lady. *The Talk of the Town* became a Las Vegas casino-type venue along the lines of *Caesar's Palace*. It attracted an impressive list of regular patrons as well. The rich and the powerful. Men at the top of their profession.'

'How wonderful. I had no idea you'd led such an exciting life.'

'It wasn't all glitz and glamour, believe you me. Long hours, rehearsals all day and the shows at night. No time for anything like a social life. Mind you I can't complain. It's where I met my first husband.'

'Did he work there too?' I asked.

She shook her head and giggled. 'He was a regular member of the audience. Every Wednesday and Friday night without fail. He used to send flowers to the stage door for me and then he started sending notes asking me to join him for a drink in the bar after the show. I ignored them for a while, and then one of the other girls persuaded me to accept. What was the worst that could happen? He was a good bit older than me, but he was tall, distinguished-looking, and great company. After a week or two he'd take me on to the casino. One thing led to another. We had twenty-four very happy years together, and he left me very well provided for.'

'Did you stay in show business?' I asked.

'Oh no. When my contract at *The Talk of the Town* came to an end, I realised the entertainment world was changing, and my stage career would be on a downward spiral from that point on. Jack persuaded me to give it up. He said we should leave London, and both make a fresh start. He had made his money as a gambler, mostly as a poker player. He bought this club down in Brighton. It was a small private establishment with a bar where you could get a meal and it had a roulette wheel. Anyway, enough about me. What about you, Graham? How did you get into giving lectures on board a cruise ship?'

'Pure chance really, I suppose. An ex-colleague from the university had been doing it for quite a few years and just before I retired, he suggested I might like to try it. Amanda and I had been cruising a few times and enjoyed it, so I decided to give it a go. He gave my details to his agency and here I am.'

'What a great way to spend your retirement.'

'We've been lucky enough to be accepted for three or four each year.'


Once the meal was over, the three of us went to the bar where Mona insisted on buying the first round of drinks.

'I always get the drinks package when I come on board.'

We spent a very enjoyable evening talking about the good old days and the various places we'd visited on our cruises. Most of the time, Mona regaled us with amusing stories of her showbiz days. I was laughing so much that my stomach was beginning to ache by the time we called it a night and went our separate ways.

'I can see why you like her so much. She's a real character, isn't she? Though I think half she says you can take with a pinch of salt,' Graham said, as we made our way to the cabin.

'You cynic,' I protested, giving him a playful punch on the arm.

'I will admit she'd be the life and soul of any party,' he said.

'Heaven knows where she gets all that energy. She must be a good ten years older than us.'

'It's a good thing that it's a sea day tomorrow and we can both have a long lie in. If you're good, I'll even make us a cup of tea in bed.'

I laughed. 'That'll be a first. I'm always awake before you.

# Day 12

At Sea

# Chapter 15

After a late breakfast on Thursday morning, Graham went back to the cabin to practise his lecture. With so many sea days on this cruise, I decided it was time to get some exercise. I've never been one for the gym. The idea of lifting weights, jumping on an exercise bike, or working on a rowing machine was my idea of purgatory. It was too cold and windy to walk around the promenade deck for laps on end with only the cold sea beneath the solid grey cloud cover to look at, so feeling restless, I decided to walk around the inside of ship where there was at least more to break the monotony.

The portside corridor ends at the open Wheelhouse Bar and as I was passing through to reach the starboard side of the ship, it was quite by chance that I spotted Sam and his wife at one of the small tables drinking coffee. As I made to go by, I caught Sam's eye and nodded. He gave me a beaming smile in return and turned to his wife.

'Julie, this is Amanda.'

She looked up. 'Hi. Sam told me how supportive you've been to him this last week.'

'I'm so sorry for your loss. It's been a difficult time for you both.'

Sam got to his feet and invited me to join them. He pulled a chair from the next table for me to sit down.

'May I just ask how you father is?' I said.

She looked a little surprised but answered readily enough, 'Much better now, thank you. They're letting him out of the infirmary this afternoon.'

'But I thought his…' I stopped myself just in time.

Sam put a reassuring hand on hers.

'It has all been rather stressful,' she said. 'Worrying about dad has stopped me thinking about mum. I don't think he's really processed her death yet. And what with everything else that's been going on…' She smiled and changed the subject. 'But everyone has been very kind. The captain has arranged for dad to have a suite up on one of the upper decks.'

'That will be nice for him.' I decided to chance my luck. 'But after what happened yesterday, I suppose he couldn't go back to his old cabin.'

'You heard about the break-in? I suppose is all over the ship by now.' Sam frowned.

'Not as far as I know. I just happened to see the door being sealed and realised it was the one next to yours.' A white lie but I decided it was best not to go into the full story. 'Was anything taken?'

'Not as far as we know. That's the ridiculous thing. Heaven knows what they were after. The place was turned upside down. The contents of all the drawers were tipped onto the floor, and they even pulled the suitcases from underneath the bed and dumped the contents on top.'

'How very odd.'

'It doesn't make sense.' Julie gave a long sigh. 'They even got into the safe. But nothing was taken. They left all Mum and Dad's money and the passports. Mum had a few bits of jewellery in there and that was there too. Why would anyone do such a thing?'

Sam patted her hand. 'Don't upset yourself love.'

'As if we haven't had enough to put up with. First Mum's death, then Dad's accident, and now this.'

'It's as though someone is out to make our lives a misery.'

It took some time to convince Graham but once I'd been able to confirm the break-in had been into Doreen and Bill's cabin, he eventually conceded there appeared to be a link between that and the fact that her handbag had been stolen.

'I'll grant you that there is a possibility that the thief didn't find what they were looking for in her handbag so broke into her cabin, but that's a long way short of saying those two things have to be connected to her death.'

'Okay, so what could they be looking for?'

'But you said that according to Julie and Sam nothing was taken from the cabin.'

'Then why did they break in?'

'Why ask me? You're the one with the obsession about all this.'

'You're the history lecturer. History is all about interpreting facts and coming to a reasonable conclusion.' I gave him my most winning smile.

'May I remind you, Amanda Mitchell, that you have the same degree as mine and you spent your whole career teaching the subject.'

'It was a very watered-down version called humanities and mostly to disinterested kids in a secondary school, whereas you, my darling, have the experience of coaching some of our brightest students who professed a passion for the subject at a university.'

'It was hardly Oxbridge!' he protested.

'Granted. But now that you are a cruise lecturer, you have developed the ability to take the bare facts and weave a story.'

'How exactly will that help solve our ship's mystery if I come up with some harebrained scenario?'

I shrugged. 'No idea but indulge me.'

'You're incorrigible!'

'I know. It's why you love me.'

He grinned, gave a long sigh. 'What do you keep in a handbag – mobile, diary, cruise card?'

'Julie didn't mention a phone. But why take that and not the cash or the jewellery? We don't know if Doreen even kept a diary. I don't suppose anyone would notice if her

97

cruise card was missing when the bag was found again, but if the thief wanted it to break into her room, why did they wait almost a week before using it?'

'So that no one would realise that the two things wouldn't be connected,' he suggested.

'I wish I knew if it was missing.'

'Amanda! Seriously, please don't go around asking questions. I'm not convinced that there is a murderer at large on the ship, but it would be downright dangerous for you to start poking your nose in.'

'Point taken.'

# Chapter 16

'Congratulations, David. That was a great lecture,' I said, once he'd finished packing up his laptop.

'I'm glad you enjoyed it.'

'I'm certainly going to try your technique of making a short video clip. The one you showed of a close up shot of the water tumbling over the rocks, then pulling back to show the stream under the bridge and finally the church was truly amazing. I can't believe you did all that with just your phone,' I said.

'The trick is to walk backwards really slowly keeping the phone steady.'

By the time we had finished chatting, everyone else had left the theatre.

'Do you two fancy a coffee?' asked Graham. 'I'd love to have a chat with you about cameras. I'm thinking about buying a new one, but the market changes so rapidly, and despite all the hype I'm never sure that the newer models are really any improvement on the old. The websites are useless because you can never find the information you need, so it's impossible to compare like with like between the different makes and models.'

As David and Graham made their way up to the theatre doors, Gwen and I followed in their wake.

'Men and their toys.' Gwen raised her eyes in mock exasperation.

The nearest place to get coffee was the Wheelhouse Bar along the corridor on the same deck. As the two men sat at the table poring over David's laptop, discussing the relative merits of cameras, Gwen and I took the more comfortable padded bench seat that curled around the corner of the room.

It wasn't long before our coffees arrived, and we had to shuffle things around on the small table to make room for the four cups and saucers. David pushed his laptop to one side and Gwen's book fell to the floor. As she was picking it up, an envelope dropped out and fluttered underneath the table. I bent to pick it up, but she quickly snatched it from my grasp and thrust it back between the pages before sitting up again.

'Damn. I've lost my place now.' She thumped the book down on the seat beside her.

After a moment or two of embarrassed silence, I tried to break the ice and said, 'How are you both enjoying cruising life? I seem to remember David saying this is your first time on board.'

'It's his first lecturing cruise but we have done a couple before, though with a different cruise line, but we're both enjoying it immensely.' She smiled, her irritation now vanished. 'David's still nervous about standing up on stage in a theatre. It's a bit different to talking in a hall somewhere to just thirty to forty people at a time or running an online workshop, but he's hoping the company will offer him other cruises in the future.'

Gwen was a friendly, sociable type who was easy to talk to. Like me, she had been a teacher before taking early retirement although she had taught seven-year-olds. We both missed the children and the classroom but were only too thankful to leave behind the reams of paperwork and report filling that had escalated over our careers. It wasn't long before the subject of the previous day's break-in crept into the conversation.

'Margaret was asking me if I'd heard any more details. We passed each other in the corridor when David and I were going up to breakfast. She seems quite obsessed with it.

Apparently, she'd already been to check if the tape was still across the door,' Gwen said.

'And is it?'

Gwen nodded. 'Anyone would think she's worried someone will break into her cabin, the way she was going on about it. But, as I told her, we don't even know for sure that's what happened. We all jumped to that conclusion yesterday but when you think about it, the door wasn't damaged. It could just as easily be a problem like a leak in the bathroom causing damage.'

'Quite possibly,' I agreed. Even though I knew what had really happened, I wasn't about to share. 'If she mentions it to me, I'll tell her the same and hopefully that might put her mind at rest.' And stop her spreading more speculation around the passengers, I thought.

Richard Jarret was in his customary spot sitting on one of the easy chairs overlooking the Atrium Lounge two decks below. I'd spotted him there a couple of times before. He looked relaxed enough, sat back with one knee nonchalantly crossed over the other, a book balanced on top. Even without the suit and tie, the white shirt didn't exactly scream 'passenger,' even if it was unbuttoned at the neck. Presumably, if he was from head office as rumour had it or, as I believed, a policeman, surely, he would have been allocated an office somewhere. Space was always tight on a ship, but no doubt some junior member of staff had been booted out of his cubbyhole and made to share with someone else. So, why wasn't he in there right now trying to get to the bottom of all that was happening? Talking to people. Checking facts. Sorting through evidence.

I must have lingered too long playing through the questions in my mind, because he caught my eye as I walked along the corridor on the far side of the vast space down to the floor of the atrium two decks below. He raised a hand in acknowledgement and smiled. I smiled back and hurried on until I was in the library and out of his eyeline.

One of the wing-backed chairs by the window was empty. It was one of my favourite spots to read. Its big enough for me to tuck my feet under me and curl up. I spent ten minutes re-reading the next few pages of *Lady Emily and the Masked Ball* but none of it had gone in.

I snapped off my Kindle and closed the case.

It was all Richard Jarret's fault, I thought crossly. If I hadn't spotted him when I was coming here, it wouldn't have brought everything back to mind. Julie had said that nothing had been taken after the break-in, but how could she be certain? Perhaps Doreen's husband might have a better idea, but presumably he hadn't been back to check – not if he was still in the medical centre. If only I could ask Richard Jarret if there were any plans for him to do so. I was less apprehensive about approaching Sam but there was a definite limit to what I could ask. It would be a big mistake to let slip any of the things I'd discovered or ask a question that might make him suspicious. Plus of course, I'd promised the captain not to discuss finding the body with anyone. Not that I cared two hoots for the captain and his orders, but I owed it to Graham not to do anything that might jeopardise any future lecture cruises that he could be offered.

# Day 13

*Narsarsuaq, Greenland*

*Narsarsuaq lies on a large area of flat land near the head of the Tunulliarfik Fjord. The long fjord juts deep into the mainland only a few miles from Greenland's permanent ice sheet. This is an area where the Viking explorers first settled because of the comparative warmth of its sheltered inland environment. Despite its tiny size – at the last census its population was 123 – it has a thriving tourist industry during its limited summer season based on the diversity of flora, its proximity to the edge of the icesheet and its history as an American air base during WWII.*

*Modern day Narsarsuaq was founded as an American air base known as Bluie West 1 in 1941. Thousands of planes used the base as a stepping-stone on their way from the aircraft factories in North America to the battlegrounds of Europe.*

*Today the old runway is used by the tiny modern airport and one of only two airports in the whole of Greenland capable of serving large airliners on international routes between Denmark and Iceland.*

*Close to the Airport, there is a unique Arctic botanical garden known as the Greenlandic Arboretum.*

Extract from the Cygnet Daily

# Chapter 17

'Wait for me,' I protested as I tried to keep up with Graham who was mounting the stairs two at a time.

'Meet you at the top,' he said over his shoulder.

'It's alright for you. I've only got short legs and do twice as many steps as you,' I protested once I'd caught my breath after the long haul to join him.

'What's the problem, old girl? These early mornings getting to you?'

'Less of the old. No need to rub it in. And as for early starts, we are supposed to be on holiday. We're never up and dressed by this time when we're back home.'

'If you're shattered already, what are you going to be like by tonight? We've got a busy day ahead of us with one tour in the morning and another in the afternoon.'

I gave a mock groan. 'I must've been mad to agree to do both.'

The Ocean Café was far from crowded, but I decided I needed a sit-down after the effort of trying to keep up with him. 'You go and get yourself something to eat and I'll try and find us a table by the window.'

I was still looking at the view by the time he joined me.

'I can see the airfield, but there's only a few houses dotted over there.'

Graham stared out to where I was pointing. 'Well, Paul did say in his port talk that Narsarsuaq only had a tiny population.'

'By the looks of things, there's not much to see. Ten

minutes and you've walked the whole village.'

'That is why you are going on a boat to the icefield to see the glacier and I'm doing a hike up Signal Hill. But my darling, neither of us will be going anywhere if you don't shift yourself and go and get your breakfast.'

By the time I returned with my bowl of fresh fruit, not only had the waiter brought a pot of tea and glasses of orange juice but two more people had joined our table and were chatting to Graham.

'Are you both on a tour this morning?' I asked as I sat down.

'We're going to visit the museum over by the airfield,' said the woman. 'Derek used to be in the Royal Air Force so he's keen to see the Bluie-West One American base. They have all sorts of old wartime equipment. Not sure if it's really my sort of thing but we'll see.'

'They do have a section which is all about the original Norse settlers plus information about all the flora and fauna of the area,' I said. 'We're planning on going there this afternoon.'

The couple went off to get their breakfast and by the time they'd returned, Graham and I were almost ready to leave.

'Have a nice day.'

'You too.'


Narsarsuaq was another tender port, and I could see the Cygnet Line awning already set up on the high quayside as our small boat sped over the choppy waves. The closer our approach, the higher the pier appeared to be.

'I wonder where we're heading,' said the woman sitting next to me. 'There's the Cygnet tent right on the top straight ahead but I can't see a landing pontoon below. How on earth are we supposed to get up that cliff face?'

'Exactly what I was thinking,' I said. 'And I can't see any sign of these small fishing boats that are supposed to be taking us to the icefield at the head of the fjord.'

Our questions were answered a few minutes later when

the tender rounded the end of the pier and turned into a small, protected bay full of the promised vessels and an obvious docking point with a long flight of steps leading to the top of the promontory. Groups of people were already filling the small vessels a hundred yards further along the quayside.

It was a slow process getting the hundred or so passengers out of the tender and up the steep narrow steps. I was one of the last to reach the top, by which time a good half of the new arrivals who had opted for the hike, were already heading for the waiting guides holding up their numbered paddles.

Kirsten, the cruise director and Liam, the excursions manager were busy attempting to marshal those going on the icefield tour into the semblance of a queue. It was proving a difficult task as everyone bunched together to keep out of the keen wind sweeping across the promontory. Several had already disappeared inside the three-sided awning and were drinking cups of hot chocolate being served by the waiters from the two big urns on the table.

My role as an escort was now pretty superfluous, I decided. Apart from leading the thirty or so passengers from the theatre to the tender boat on the lowest deck, my job was at an end. Each of the fishing boats could only accommodate eight or so people at a time which meant that we were now being divided into small groups, and I would accompany the last one.

'Are you going to see the glacier too?'

I turned to see Mona's smiling face half-hidden in the fur-lined hood of her padded jacket.

'Oh hi! I didn't recognise you at first.'

'I hope this is all going to be worth it. It's flipping freezing out here.' Her hearty chortle had me smiling too.

'I'm sure it will be.'

Together we joined the end of the queue. Despite the apparent chaos, things moved relatively quickly.

'Our esteemed Kirsten is a wonder, isn't she?' said Mona.

'When she gets any sleep, heaven knows. She was up in the Sky Lounge compering the late-night cabaret last night and here she is next morning up at the crack of dawn in time to catch the first tender to set up all this. She's there first thing every morning with a smile to greet the passengers and then again long after midnight always the last to leave. She may be a spring chicken compared to us, but how anyone can keep going, seven days a week for months on end, is anyone's guess.'

'I expect she goes back to bed in the middle of the day, but I agree, it takes a special sort of person to be a cruise director. And you're one to talk about burning the candle at both ends. I take it you were up at the karaoke yourself last night.'

'Only till about half past ten.'

'With Tony? How's it going between you and our chaplain?'

Her smile faded. 'It's not. I haven't seen him for a few days. At least not to talk to. He hasn't been to any of the late-night entertainment since the formal evening. I spotted him at the bar as I walked through the lounge yesterday. I waved, but either he didn't see me or he's avoiding me.'

There wasn't much to say in answer to that, so it was a good thing that we were ushered down to the waiting fishing boat.


A collective gasp followed the whoosh of sound as a huge chunk of ice suddenly broke away from the face of the glacier and plunged into the sea below. Hastily, we all grabbed the side of the boat and held on as the resulting waves raced towards us.

'That was amazing!' Mona's face was a picture of smiles as the tiny vessel bobbed like a cork riding the buffeting swells. 'Did you get a photo?'

I shook my head. 'Not as it splashed into the sea.'

'I think I got one,' said a man sitting opposite who was busy looking at the screen on the back of his camera. 'Not as good as I hoped.'

He leant across to show us.

'How about you?'

All eyes turned to the man standing with his back wedged against the front of the wheelhouse, sporting an obviously expensive camera with a four-inch lens. He too was reviewing his latest shots. It was about thirty seconds before he looked up, a slow smile spreading from ear to ear. 'Managed to get a video. It's not bad actually.'

The skipper turned the boat and zig-zagged a path through the mass of floating ice. We spent the journey back to the quay looking at the photographer's video plus a few others of some of the more spectacular bergs that we'd passed on the way. He may not have been a professional, but his photos were excellent, and he promised he would email the rest of us with a copy of the video of the carving glacier as it crashed into the sea.

Both Mona and I had been too excited to notice the cold while we were on the tiny fishing boat but once we'd climbed the steps back onto the top, we felt the chill.

'My fingers are frozen even with thick gloves.' Mona shook her hands trying to get back the circulation.

'Hot chocolate next, I think,' I said, and we headed to the awning.

Two minutes later, each clutching our paper cups like a mini hot water bottle, we tagged onto the end of the queue for the next tender back to the *Sea Dream*.

Mona cuddled her cup against her cheek. 'That's better.'

'I want to hear more about your glamourous past.'

'I told you the other night, it really wasn't like that. Even *The Talk of the Town* had its seamy side.'

'Oh, do tell!' I was agog.

'When I started, like all new girls, I was warned not to mess with the punters on certain tables. I don't claim they were mafia exactly, though for all I know some may well have been, but let's say they operated on the fringes of the underworld.'

'Opening a private club down in Brighton sounds pretty glamourous to me. Did you sing there?'

'It wasn't that sort of club. No entertainment. Just a private club where you could get a drink, a meal and a flutter. Jack invited some of his London friends to *The Albion* when it first opened, people I knew, at least by sight from *The Talk of the Town*.'

'None of the bad guys, I hope.'

'Well, there was one, that I confess I didn't take to. I'm not saying he was part of the criminal fraternity, but everyone called him Mr Smith, though I doubt that was his real name. Anyway, this Mr Smith often brought a few other people with him I hadn't seen before. Jack never talked much about his business dealings though he claimed he'd always made his money legally, but I wonder if this Smith had lent Jack some of the money to buy *The Albion* and had a stake in the business. I won't say he was a regular, but he'd pop into the club two or three times a year and the two always disappeared into Jack's private office for half an hour after he and his cronies had had their meal.'

# Chapter 18

Both Graham and I prefer to sleep in a cool bedroom, and, because we're always forgetting to adjust the air conditioning controls, our cabin is by no means the warmest place on the ship. I divested myself of my outdoor gear and decided that the earlier small cup of hot chocolate had whetted my appetite for more. Graham wasn't due back for at least another half hour which left me plenty of time to go to the coffee station in the library to get a decent sized mug from the machine.

There was no one else in the library to talk to and I'd forgotten to bring anything to read. I sat down but after five minutes, I felt restless. Neither of us had collected that day's sudoku and the newssheet from reception so, drinking down the last of the chocolate, I returned my mug to the counter, and made my way to the rear staircase.

Richard Jarret was sitting in his customary position overlooking the atrium.

'Either the powers that be haven't found you an office to work in or you are treating your time on board as a holiday.' I couldn't resist the dig.

He looked up and smiled. 'Mrs Mitchell. Amanda. And good morning to you, too.' The hazel eyes twinkled.

I grinned back, resting my hands on the back of the chair facing him across the small low drinks table.

'To answer your question, I am actually working.' He nodded to the pile of papers on his knee. 'I have been given an office, but it is rather small and doesn't have a window which is why, once in a while, I choose to sit out here where I find it easier to think.'

'I see.' I decided to push my luck. 'I've been doing some thinking too.'

'Oh?'

'I was wondering if there was a possible connection between Doreen's stolen handbag and someone breaking into her cabin?'

His left eyebrow rose a fraction, then he smiled and said casually, 'Has there been a break-in?'

I wanted to say, *'You know darn well there has. You were there!'*, but despite his goading, I smiled and replied. 'Her daughter Julie mentioned it.'

He wagged a finger at me. 'Mrs Mitchell, I thought you were asked not to discuss Mrs Bowland with any of the other passengers.'

'I was told not to talk about her death. Which I haven't. I know about the break-in because I saw Julie and her husband the other day and asked after her father as I learnt he had had a fall. She happened to mention that someone had let themselves into his cabin and searched the place.' I sank down into the chair facing him and gave him a steady glare. I was not going until I had an answer.

'I see.'

'It must have crossed your mind that the two events must be connected.'

'I see you have been doing some detective work of your own…'

'So you *are* a policeman,' I said triumphantly.

He gave a low chuckle. 'I didn't say that Mrs Mitchell. But I'd be interested in hearing your thoughts as to what, if anything, an intruder might have been after.'

'Julie mentioned that as far as she could tell, nothing was taken…' I took a deep breath.

'Go on.'

'Given that the burglar ignored the cash and valuables, it would seem logical to assume that he was after something specific. Presumably, as the family were not aware of anything that was missing, the conclusion is that it had to be something that the rest of the family didn't know about. Something that wouldn't be missed.'

'You've lost me.'

'Something that didn't belong to her in the first place.'

He frowned. I'd clearly piqued his interest because the gently mocking tone was gone when he said, 'Such as?'

'I've no idea. Something small because no one in her family could have noticed it.'

'Would they, if she'd hidden it?'

'True, but let's face it, there are very few places in a cabin where you can hide something when you're sharing it with someone else. Besides, why would the thief look for it in her handbag?'

He sat back and tapped his lips with his index finger.

I let the silence hang for what seemed an age until I could bear it no longer. 'So, what do you think?'

He looked up at me. 'I think, Mrs Mitchell, that you need to spend far less time trying to concoct fanciful theories out of a series of events which may well be totally unconnected.'

I gripped the arms of the chair digging my nails into the padded upholstery.

'But whatever the thief was looking for, has to be the key to the murder,' I blurted out.

'Mrs Mitchell!'

Now I'd blown it. I hadn't meant to antagonise the one person with whom I'd built up some sort of rapport. Someone who was prepared to listen to my theories and more importantly someone from whom I might learn more details that would make sense of the three seemingly unrelated events.

'I'm sorry. I shouldn't have bothered you.'

I got to my feet and turned to leave, but he seized my wrist.

'I do understand that finding a dead body in such appalling circumstances must be a very distressing experience and that you feel the need to make sense of what happened, but please Mrs Mitchell, under no circumstances should you start asking questions. At best you could cause all sorts of panic to spread amongst the passengers and at worst, if there is the remotest chance that any of what you believe should prove to be true, you could put yourself in danger.'

I nodded and tried to pull my hand away, but his grip was still firm.

'Do I make myself clear?'

I nodded again but only when I'd replied out loud, did he release me.

# Chapter 19

My interview with Richard Jarret had shaken me to the core. So much so that I couldn't even tell Graham about it. I did my best to make the right noises over lunch when he talked excitedly about his excursion.

'Did you know that the area around Narsarsuaq is the only place in the whole of Greenland where trees can be grown?' He popped a forkful of macaroni cheese into his mouth.

'Really?'

'The last thing I expected to see were the flowers. And not just the odd few. There were masses of them. And so many different varieties and vibrant colours. Some I recognised like harebells, buttercups, ox-eye daisies, and purple saxifrage, but there were no end of pretty little pink ones clinging to the rocks and great stretches of artic cotton grass which looked like little tufts of cottonwool stuck on spikes poking out of the grass. I took lots of pictures. I'll show you when we get back to the cabin.'

He pushed away his empty plate and waited for me to finish the last of my salad.

'You must tell me all about your morning, but first I'm going to get myself a dessert. Are you going to have one?'

'I think I'll stick to some cheese and a couple of digestive biscuits, if I can find any.'

I was feeling much more like my old self by the time we left to catch the tender back to the quay to visit the museum. I enjoyed the museum far more than I thought I would. The stuff about the planes, the radio equipment and other technical gizmos didn't really grab my attention, but I enjoyed the room made up to resemble a ward in the old station hospital with a bed, bits of equipment and plenty of photographs pinned on the walls. I left Graham and wandered on to read the information about the arrival of Erik the Red and the Vikings settlers. The life-sized models were well worth a picture or two.

'Amazing to think that four thousand men were stationed here at the height of the war. The whole complex must have been huge,' Graham said as we came out of the building pulled his gloves out of his pocket. 'Shall we go and look at the statue?'

The life-size granite statue in the centre of the grassy square in front of the building represented Erik the Red bending down from the saddle to lift his son Leif onto his horse with his wife holding the animal's head to keep it steady.

'So much for putting your gloves on again,' I joked as he pulled them off and handed them to me to hold so he could take photos.

I'd already wandered off to look more closely at some of the wildflowers in the waste ground at the side of the museum by the time he'd finished.

'I'm not sure you'll really need these,' I said as I handed back the gloves.

We had caught the small bus from the quayside to bring us to the museum but decided to stroll back along the flat plain with the scattered houses on one side and the runway on the other. We stopped every now and again to look at the small clumps of wildflowers by the side of the path.

'It's considerably warmer this afternoon,' I said. 'It was downright icy on the water this morning. The wind cut right through you.'

Graham laughed. 'Then you should have climbed up Signal Hill with me. Several of our lot took their coats off on the way back down they got so warm.'

'Sez you.'

'Would I lie to you?'

I still wasn't convinced, but I will admit the walk back was pleasantly warm as I lifted my face to the sun.

'I don't think I've been this warm outside since we left Kirkwall,' I said.

'We are considerably further south than Nuuk. And Iceland, come to that. This is supposed to be the warmest part of Greenland. It's why the Viking colonists first settled here.'

I gave him a playful punch. 'Save the history for your lecture. This is your wife you're talking to.'

'Would you mind sharing a table this evening?'

'No problem.'

The young woman at the desk signalled a waiter to escort us to our table where a man was already sitting. He looked up from his menu and smiled as the waiter pulled out my chair, picked up the linen napkin, deftly flicked it across my lap and handed me my menu.

I recognised our fellow diner even without his dog collar. 'Good evening. It's Reverend Parker-Scott, isn't it?'

He looked momentarily surprised and glanced at Graham shuffling his chair under the table.

'Please call me Tony.'

'Graham and Amanda Mitchell.'

'Of course. You're the history lecturer.' He turned back to me. 'Now I recognise your face. We shook hands at that preliminary meeting, though I confess I didn't remember your name. May I say how attractive you are looking this evening. That pink blouse suits your colouring.'

There was a pause in the conversation while Graham and I studied our menus, followed by an embarrassed silence as we tried to think of something to say. Thankfully, we were soon joined by an elderly gentleman with clipped moustache and bushy white eyebrows. He was smartly dressed in a tweed jacket and striped tie and introduced himself as Clive.

'I'm very bad at remembering names, but I will remember yours because I had a cousin with the same name,' said Tony.

'Have you been on the ship before?' I asked the newcomer.

It was Clive's third time on the *Sea Dream* and once he had sung the ship's praises, he asked Tony how long he'd been a ship's chaplain.

'This is my first time doing this sort of thing, and I'm still learning the ropes so to speak. Cruising is a great way to see new places, isn't it? I've never been to Iceland or Greenland before.'

'I always think the included excursion is a great way to get a first taste of the place if you're new to the port,' said Clive.

'I agree. I think Graham and I have enjoyed all the excursions on offer that we've ever done. Have you tried any of the excursions yet, Tony?'

'I have a friend who lives in Kirkwall, so I spent the day with him in our first port. To be honest, I prefer to explore places on my own rather than being taken somewhere with a large group of other people.'

Before long, the conversation turned to family. Clive had been a widower for over twenty years and his only son had emigrated to New Zealand.

'We keep in touch. He keeps inviting me to go over there for a holiday, but at my age I just can't face travelling halfway across the world.' He turned to Tony. 'I take it that you're not married?'

'No. I don't have any family. I was an only child and since my cousin died three months ago, I'm quite alone in the world. Not that we ever saw a great deal of each other. That said, we crossed paths in Switzerland in the spring just before he died.'

The waiter cleared away our dessert plates and asked if we would like coffee.

Clive looked at his watch. 'Not for me. I'd like to go to the show tonight. It's the magician and I'd like to get a seat near the front.'

'He's a pleasant old boy. Bit old school, stiff upper lip and all that. He didn't say, but penny to a pound he was in the army,' said Tony, as we watched the retreating upright figure.

'I wouldn't mind seeing the magician either.' Graham turned to me. 'Do you fancy it? We've got time if we don't linger over coffee.'

'Fine by me. How about you, Tony. Care to join us?'

'Not my thing, I'm afraid.'

'So, are you heading up to the late-night bar later on?'

He shook his head and smiled benignly. 'I don't think so.'

'Really. I heard you were the highlight of the karaoke and then made quite an impression on the dance floor.'

His eyes widened and he gave an uncomfortable smile.

'I did rather let myself get carried away one night.' Recovering his easy charm, he continued, 'I haven't always been a vicar. Truth to tell, I led quite a wild youth. A bit of a rebel until I joined the ministry and changed my riotous ways.'

'Have you been ordained long?'

'Only a few years.'

Graham drank the last of his coffee. 'Time we were going if we want to catch the show, Amanda.'

We bade Tony good night and left.

'That went better than I thought it might,' said Graham, as I tried to match my steps to his as he strode down the corridor. 'My heart dropped a bit when I saw the chaplain sitting at the table. After seeing him at the Sunday Service, I wasn't quite sure what to expect. Still think he's too smarmy by half, but perhaps that's just me.'

'He does lay the charm on a bit thick.'

'What was that about the karaoke?'

'Mona mentioned that's where she met him. The way she talked about him; you'd think she was referring to a totally different person.'

# Day 14

*Nanortalik, Greenland*

*Nanortalik is Greenland's most southerly town and lies on a small island near the mouth of the Tasermiut Fjord. The area was one of the first parts of Greenland to be settled by the Vikings. The town grew up in the eighteenth century as a permanent trading depot.*

*The name Nanortalik is the Greenlandic for "The Place where the Polar Bear goes," and although polar bears are supposed to live and hunt on the sea ice offshore, they are rarely seen here.*

*The town is home to just over 1,500 people which makes it Greenland's tenth largest town.*

Extract from the Cygnet Daily

# Chapter 20

'Wouldn't it be great to see a polar bear?'

Graham looked up from his cornflakes and raised his eyebrows. 'It'll be a miracle if we did. Wrong time of year anyway.'

I pulled a face. 'I know that. But we might just see a whale. Minke whales are supposed to be common visitors to the fjord. They even get the odd humpback and orca.'

'You'll be lucky.'

'Don't be such a misery. Go and get yourself a Danish pastry and sweeten yourself up.'

He gave me a cheesy grin. 'Do you want anything?'

'I'm good, thanks.'

I'd finished my second cup of tea by the time he'd returned.

'I'll go back to the cabin and clean my teeth while you finish then we won't be fighting for the bathroom at the same time,' I said.

'Okeydokey. See you in a bit.'

I threaded my way between the tables, not the easiest of tasks with so many people popping back and forth from the serving area, and I spotted Mona tucking into an English breakfast with all the works.

'Hello.'

She looked up and quickly wiped away the dribble of egg yolk from her chin. 'Hi there, Amanda. Are you escorting this morning?'

'They don't need anyone today because it's an open tour.

Once the tender drops us all off, we're free to visit the various places and watch the activities on, on our own. I take it you're going to go ashore?'

'Oh yes. We're off this afternoon.'

'We? Who are you going with this time?'

'I sat with this charming chap called Alastair at dinner last night. I happened to mention that the only thing I didn't like about the tours was when we're given free time. I'm always worried I'll get lost and can't find my way back to the meeting point. I've got no sense of direction. Then he very kindly offered to accompany me.'

'Knowing you, the poor chap probably didn't have much option.'

She giggled. 'Don't worry, I'll be sure to treat him to a drink or two in one of the local bars as a thank you.'

Her smile suddenly changed to a frown.

'Something wrong?' I glanced over my shoulder to catch what she'd been looking at.

'No, nothing like that. You know how you see somebody, and they remind you of someone from your past? You know it can't be them, but…' she shook her head.

'It's upset you.'

'Not really.' She gave me a broad smile. 'It's just one of those silly coincidences. It probably wouldn't have happened at all if I hadn't told you about the Albion Club and Mr Smith yesterday. Every now and again, Mr Smith would invite us to a show in London and then take us on to a casino. The last time we went, there was this younger chap who was some sort of runner. Not one of his heavies. He was a bit pathetic actually. Always trying to ingratiate himself with the boss. Desperate to get in on the action.'

'And you think he's here on the ship?'

'Heaven's no. Something about him just reminded me of this young chap twenty odd years ago. I only saw him the once and never thought about him since.'

'And this person you saw just now; was he a passenger?'

'No, he was one of your lot.' She laughed. 'You'll never

guess who…'

'Excuse me. Are these seats taken?'

Mona and I both turned to the rather impatient looking man who had appeared next to me holding a plate of kippers in one hand and glass of orange juice in the other.

'Go ahead. I'm not stopping,' I said.

At this rate, I was going to be late. With a quick, 'Catch up with you later,' to Mona, I hurried to the exit. Graham was probably down in the cabin already and wondering where I'd got to.


There was a display board a hundred yards from the Cygnet awning which gave details of all the activities taking place throughout the day.

'We've just missed the kayak display at 9 o'clock, but the choir are doing a performance in the church in half an hour. Do you fancy that?' Graham orientated the town map we'd been given. 'It's over in that direction, just before you get to the old colonial harbour.'

'Fine by me.'

The white wooden church lay at the top of a gently ascending path to the south of the town and in no time at all we spotted the red roof on the tall tower at one end of the building. We arrived early which gave Graham plenty of time to take copious pictures not only of the pretty little church but also the vast carpets of yellow buttercups outside.

'I don't think I've ever seen so many all-in-one place,' I said. 'The whole landscape seems to be covered in them.

Graham was still clicking away five minutes later.

'I'll go in and get a seat.'

'Be there in a sec,' he said, without looking up from his crouched position near the ground trying to get closeup shots.

Knowing him, I didn't hold out much hope. The inside of the small church was simple and unadorned – a legacy from the time of Hans Egede, the eighteenth century Danish-

Norwegian Lutheran missionary.

The choir members were already beginning to assemble. The women were dressed in what looked like red Fair Isle sweaters, black trousers and long white boots with fancy patterned tops. The men looked quite dull by comparison in plain white tops and black trousers.

Many of the songs they sang were hymns, though there were a few traditional folk songs. The performance was quite short and at the end we all trooped out with the dozen or so choir members to take photos. Several of the audience had their pictures taken with the choir but I've never liked having my picture taken so declined the opportunity. I did however get the chance to see the national costumes up close. What I'd thought was a knitted pattern on the women's woollen sweaters turned out to be an elaborate beaded collar that covered the upper arms and chest of a red silk tunic. Each collar was a different pattern with red, white, black, and blue beads. The amount of work involved must have been enormous, not only on the collars but the patches on their trousers and the fancy lacy tops to their thigh-high boots. One of the locals explained that men's snow-white tops were made of sealskin.

I moved back out of the way to give more room to the photographers and that was when I spotted Margaret standing at the corner of the church.

'Did you see the little concert?'

She shook her head. 'Sadly no. We spent too long in the harbour watching a man rolling his canoe over and righting it again. Very impressive. When we realised the time, we knew we'd miss the beginning, but we thought we'd catch the end.'

'It only lasted twenty minutes or so. There is another performance in a couple of hours.'

I looked around for Paul and spotted him taking photos. Margaret and I chatted for a while, but she soon became fidgety.

'I do wish Paul would hurry up. I'm getting cold just

standing around waiting.'

'That's the lot of us photographers' wives, I'm afraid. But by the looks of things the group are beginning to break up, so you won't have to wait much longer.'

The only response to my light-hearted retort was a long sigh.

Paul returned not long after with a decided scowl marring his features. He completely ignored me and glared at Margaret.

'I told you we shouldn't have spent so long in the harbour. Now we've missed the concert altogether.'

Margaret mumbled an apology.

'We might as well go in and take a look round the inside of the church now we've come all this way.' Without waiting for a reply, Paul turned and marched towards the short flight of wooden steps with Margaret trotting behind like a faithful dog following its master.

'What's that sour expression for? You look as though you've just caught a whiff of something very unpleasant.'

Graham's voice made me start. I hadn't noticed him joining me.

'Actually, you're not far wrong. The more I see of that man, the less I like him,' I muttered more to myself than Graham.

'Who are we talking about?'

'Paul.'

'Really? He seems nice enough to me. He was certainly very helpful showing me all sorts of tricks on PowerPoint the other day.'

'It's the way he treats his wife I don't like. Half the time, he doesn't even seem to notice that she's there. She just trails along after him. I get the impression that he makes all the decisions.'

'Can't say I've really noticed.' He tucked an arm through mine. 'So, Mrs Mitchell what would *you* like to do next?'

We strolled along the promontory to the old colonial harbour. Though we'd missed the kayak display, we both enjoyed the open-air museum, which was a collection of old houses showing what life was like for the early colonists.

When we came out of the turf house, we were met by half a dozen or so young teenagers who welcomed us to their town first in Greenlandic and then in English. They were eager to take us to their stall where they were selling homemade cakes to raise money for their school. After we'd each chosen a couple of cakes, we spent a good ten minutes chatting with them.

'Do you like living here?' Graham asked.

They enthused about the freedom they had to get out and enjoy the countryside and only one complained about the long, dark winters. We asked about their lives and what they wanted to do when they were older. Interestingly, they were nearly all happy to stay in Nanortalik. They asked us about our lives back home, about travelling on the ship and the other countries we'd been to. If we hadn't made our excuses, there was a good chance they would have kept us talking until the last tender.

'That was fun.'

Graham gave a contented sigh and took my hand as we strolled along the track towards the housing area. 'The sun is shining and just breathe in that good, clean air. No pollution. No traffic fumes. Still, I suppose there's not much point in having cars when there are no roads out of town.'

'And no tarmacked roads or decent paths in the town either,' I said in mock-annoyance, then gave him a broad grin. 'No. You're right. It is amazingly peaceful. It's great to spend a whole day together like this. We should do this more often.'

# Day 15

*Qaqortoq, Greenland*

*Qaqortoq is the largest city in South Greenland with a population of around three thousand people which makes it the island's fourth largest city. It is home to eight hundred students many of whom come from the north of the country.*

*Its steep rolling countryside is dotted with colourful houses, eighteenth century colonial buildings, and interesting stone carvings that form an outdoor museum. It is one of the only towns in Greenland that has a square, with Greenland's oldest fountain in the centre. Alongside the square is the museum housed in the town's oldest building, a black-tarred colonial administrator's house built in 1804.*

*The surrounding area has been inhabited since prehistoric times and the town itself was established by the Danish General Trading Company in 1775.*

*Even in summer, large icebergs float down the fjord from the calving glacier which lies miles to the north.*

Extract from the Cygnet Daily

# Chapter 21

The next morning the sky was overcast, and the threat of rain hung in the air. Not the best of starts for an early morning tour.

The sea was decidedly choppy, and I was more than grateful for the firm hold that the two crewmen kept on my arms as I stepped onto the bobbing tender. I paused for a second or two regaining my balance.

'Hi there.'

I turned my head to see Mona sitting at the end of the bench a few rows away beckoning me to join her. The rear of the boat looked full, but she shuffled her bottom along the seat telling the man next to her sitting with his legs spread wide to budge up.

'Are you doing the town walk and museum?' she asked.

'No. I'm on the visit to a local house.'

Her ready smile faded. 'That's a shame.'

'So how did it go with Alastair, yesterday? Did you have a good time?'

'Oh yes!' The cherubic smile was back. 'We had a great time. Quite a gentleman, and it was so nice to have someone to talk to and share the experience with as we were going round different places. You relax and enjoy yourself more when you're with someone else.'

'I know what you mean. Graham always notices things I might have missed and vice versa. But, if the two of you had such a great time together, why are you on your own today?'

'Alastair is really into history – he loves your husband's

lectures by the way, told me to tell you when I next saw you – so he opted to go on the boat trip to see the remains of a Viking church. Even to have the pleasure of his company, I draw the line at wandering round a few old ruins. Perhaps it's my lack of imagination that I can't visualise the original buildings in all their glory, but I really can't get excited about stone walls barely higher than your kneecaps, however many there are.'

'Probably best not to pass on that particular snippet to my husband,' I said with a grin. 'I don't know how many groups are on that tour, but there's a good chance Alastair and Graham are on the same one so they can enthuse together over what's left of the site. But the big question is are you and Alastair meeting up again?'

She gave me a coy look. 'Nothing specific, although we have both booked to go on the visit to the Glens when we get to Belfast, and we've agreed to make sure we go on the same coach.'

'And is there a chance of the two of you meeting up when you get home?'

She burst into laughter. 'I shouldn't think so for a moment. He's a lovely man but really not my type. Aside from the cruise, we have little in common. Apart from anything else, he lives up in Northumberland somewhere near the Scottish border and I'm on the south coast.'

The tender was rapidly approaching the shore and everyone else was gathering their belongings together ready to disembark. Time to prepare to face the cold. I felt in my pockets.

'Oh no! I must have left my gloves behind. I shall just have to keep my hands in my pockets when I'm outside.'

'No problem.' She pulled her tote bag onto her lap and rooted around inside. 'Here you are. I always carry a spare pair just in case. I'm always putting my gloves down somewhere and leaving them behind.'

She handed me the gloves.

'You're a star. I'll return them as soon as we're back on

the ship.'

'No hurry. Let me have them when you see me. We've got two days at sea before we get to our next port and our paths are bound to cross at some point.'

'Why don't we meet for coffee tomorrow morning, and I can give them to you then?'

'I'd love that.'

'Say ten-thirty, in the Wheelhouse Bar.'

'See you then.'


Acting as a tender, the ship's lifeboats can hold somewhere between a hundred-and-twenty to a hundred-and-fifty people and ours was packed to capacity, so it took some time to offload everyone. Kirsten and several members of the shore excursions team in their cherry red anoraks were waiting under the awning ready to point us all in the right direction to find our guides. My group were gathering at the top of a gentle rise.

'The skies are beginning to brighten up,' I said to the couple next to me.

'That's a relief. I thought we might get some rain when I looked out first thing.'

The forty-odd people who had opted for the home visit were divided into four smaller groups. I joined the last one. Our guide was a tall good-looking, middle-aged man with fair hair and of obvious Danish origin. Whether his family dated back to the late-eighteenth century when the town was founded as a trading post for the Danish owned General Trading Company, he didn't say, but it was clear that his family roots went back for some time.

We set off up the steep path that climbed the hillside and wound its way past the closely packed colourful wooden houses all painted in bright primary colours. Even after a couple of hundred yards, the crocodile had become strung out. I joined a woman struggling at the back.

'You have to be fit to live here,' she said, as she paused holding onto a fence to catch her breath.

'Take your time,' I said. 'No rush. The others have all stopped anyway. They're busy taking photos so you're not holding up anyone.'

The views were picturesque, and we were high enough to be able to look down onto the harbour and see our ship anchored in the narrow bay. In the other direction the houses crowded onto the hillside, each on its own small patch of levelled ground with a short set of steps to the narrow paths that twined between them.

Once we were all together again, the guide began his spiel telling us about the town's history and the trade in whale and seal skins, blubber and meat.

'If you look over there, can you see the white building with a large seal painted on it? That's the tannery.'

We made slow progress up the hill, partly because people kept stopping to take photos and because our guide made frequent stops, ostensibly to give us a few more snippets of information, but I suspect it was mainly because we had two or three people who were finding the steep climb a bit of a struggle.

We had been in Greenland long enough to appreciate that the tourist season is very short, and the guides we'd had so far had other jobs for the rest of the year. It was almost inevitable that eventually someone would ask the question.

He gave a slow smile. 'I spend most of the year in America. I'm the Greenland Ambassador for America. Officially, I'm over here on holiday for the summer but my wife is the port agent in charge of all the tours for the cruise ships, and she ropes me in when she's short of guides.'

One of the other home visit groups overtook us while we were stopped, and I noticed another further ahead peel off onto a side road. Eventually, our guide pointed to a house on our right clinging to the hillside.

'Not too far now everyone. Do you see the bright green house up there? That's where we're heading.'

'Thank goodness for that,' muttered the backmarker I'd stayed with.

'Do you need to stop for a breather?'

She gave a long sigh and leant on a post, breathing heavily. She unwound the scarf from around her neck and unbuttoned the thick navy jacket she was wearing.

'It's getting warm, isn't it?' She fanned her face with the end of her scarf.

I smiled sympathetically. The tour had been classified as severe on the excursion details, but I thought it tactful not to mention it. It was the age-old problem that Graham always moaned about. Whatever the context, people never bothered to read the details carefully and when it came to the ship excursions there was a tendency for older passengers to over-estimate their ability and levels of fitness.

'Take your time. There's no rush. We know where we're going.'

I took the opportunity to survey the scenery. There were a couple of men deep in conversation some fifty or so yards down the path that veered off to our left. The one facing me pushed back his hood and I thought for a moment that I recognised him even at this distance. Tony had the same habit of brushing back the lock of dark hair that frequently fell across his forehead. The two men turned and walked up the steps and disappeared into the house. Presumably they were joining another of the groups on a visit to one of the local houses.

The last of our group were still removing their boots and shoes by the time I arrived with the straggler. A couple of men were taking pictures of the attractive flowers on the bank up to the house while they waited for the tiny porch to empty.

Once we'd divested ourselves of our coats, scarves and hats in the hallway, we were ushered into the living-cum-dining-room by our hostess – a tiny Inuit woman who didn't speak any English.

The table was laden with scones, small cakes and a variety of delicacies. It was a tight squeeze fitting chairs for all ten of us around it but once we were all seated, our guide introduced our hostess as Pipaluk and translated her welcome speech. Not that her invitation to tuck in needed much translation.

It was fascinating, listening about life in Greenland and how much it had changed during her lifetime. It came as a surprise to hear that the spritely woman was ninety years old.

'Pipaluk is Greenland's senior women's handball champion,' our guide announced with a touch of pride.

She held up a bandaged right hand, an injury which she sustained in a recent game. Her broken finger made it difficult to put on her national dress, but she had laid it out on the back of the settee and explained what material each piece was made of and how it was put together.

'Did you make it yourself?' asked one of the women.

We learnt that Inuit women usually make their own costumes, most often for their wedding day though some inherit their national dress from their grandmothers. The amount of embroidery and the beadwork can take several years to complete. The finished outfits are highly prized.

'My eldest great granddaughter will inherit mine.'

'But what about your other three granddaughters? Are you going to make costumes for them?'

Pipaluk waved a dismissive hand. 'That is for my daughters to sort out.'

Everyone wanted to take photos of the whole outfit including the long white sealskin boots with their embroidered tops.

'The leather is so soft,' said one woman who was gently stroking one of the boots. 'Is it dyed to get it so white?'

'Once the fur is removed, the skins are left outside to bleach in the snow.'


The time came for us to leave. Our hostess came to the door and stood waving as we made our way back down the hillside.

'That was a thoroughly enjoyable morning,' someone said,

and everyone agreed.

'There is nothing to stop you exploring a little more of our beautiful town on your own,' said our guide. 'If you follow the path, it will take you into the central square where you will find shops, a bakery, and the museum. You can also visit the old, red-painted wooden church built by the Danish missionaries or up on the hill the much bigger modern concrete church built in the 1970s.'

I'd noticed the half a dozen or so locals setting out their stalls alongside the wooden Welcome Centre building when we had first arrived. Inevitably, they acted as a magnet for our little group when we got back to where the tenders were operating. As we'd discovered everywhere in Greenland, the Inuit people were very friendly and were happy to tell us all about the various craft items that ranged from hand-made jewellery, crocheted items to small carved stone objects they had produced.

'They are so unusual,' I said to the woman standing next to me as I held out a black stone walrus and a bird to the man behind the stall. 'I don't normally buy souvenirs, but I'm going to get these for my children.'

'I've already bought bracelets for each of my granddaughters, but I think I'm going to get one of these for myself. I'm torn between the little Eskimo figure and the seal.'

'They are fun,' I agreed.

Now my escort duties were over, and knowing Graham wouldn't be back for a couple of hours, I decided to explore the town before returning to the ship.

The path up behind the Visitor Centre led to a collection of stone carvings on the rocky hillside. I took out my phone and snapped a few photos. There were too many to take pictures of them all, so I limited my selection to a few of my favourites – a ram's head, a collection of faces, and a group of whales. At the top of the hill, I had a great view over the fishing harbour which I decided to make my next stop.

I hadn't gone far when I spotted a supermarket. I made a

quick diversion to take a peek inside. There must have been as many of the ship's passengers as there were locals, wandering around inspecting what was on offer. The bakery items looked very tempting. Had I not had more than my fill at the home visit, I might well have succumbed.

In some respects, it resembled a supermarket back home with aisles of the usual produce although the brands were very different. But then came a section selling everything else you might need, from clothes, shoes, household goods, white goods, electrical equipment, hardware items including pails and buckets, harpoons and bits of equipment I couldn't begin to identify. The modest-sized supermarket effectively sold everything you might expect to buy in the high street shops back home under a single roof.

The fish market was not nearly as fishy smelling as I expected, but as I wandered along the line of trestle tables I saw more whale and seal meat than actual fish. It was time to be heading back but I couldn't help taking a quick diversion up to the old wooden church, not so much to see inside St. Saviour's but to take a closer look at the field of wildflowers stretching beyond it. I'd have loved to have sat down and enjoyed the peace and quiet beside the gently bubbling stream that ran alongside, but I needed to get back to the ship.

# Chapter 22

It was almost time for lunch when Graham got back from the Hvalso Norse ruins trip.

'Did you get lots of pictures?'

'Of course. Mostly of the church. It must have been quite a big farmstead to justify such a large building. We were told the present ruins replace an older, smaller chapel, so I presume the original farm grew into a much bigger settlement. Not that there was much left of the village itself, just a few stones marking the outline walls of some houses and the stables.'

'Were there many on the tour?'

'There were only eight on my boat, but another boat arrived ten minutes later. And then a couple more came just as we were leaving. We were using small fishing boats that couldn't take more than a handful of people at a time.'

'Similar to my trip to see the icefield and the glacier the other day. Those little boats are quite fun, aren't they?'

'It was a bumpy ride, but we got some fantastic views. How about the home visit, was it good?'

It was as much to keep Graham company that I said I'd go up with him to the Ocean Café for lunch than because I was hungry. I had restricted myself to a single scone and jam and a slice of cake on my home visit, but I'd probably exceeded my calories for the middle of the day.

'Everything was homemade. The jam was lovely, made from local wild berries that she'd picked when they were in season. It was an amazing spread. There's another cruise ship coming in tomorrow which meant that she was planning to spend this afternoon baking to get ready to do it all again.'

David and Gwen were coming out of their cabin when we went out, so the four of us went to eat together. We found a table by the window.

'You all go and get something to eat while I keep the seats,' I said.

'I'm starving after that hike round the lake,' said David. 'It may have only been three and a half miles but most of it was clambering over rocky stretches and rough terrain.'

Both he and Gwen who had done the same tour came back with plates piled high.

'Is that all you're having?' said David when I came back with a bowl of soup.

It was a pleasant, leisurely lunch as no one had plans for the afternoon. Our plates had long since been cleared away and the waiter had brought us all a second cup of coffee when Gwen sat back shaking her head. We all turned to see what she was looking at. Paul was walking towards the exit with Margaret trotting three or four steps behind.

'Anyone would think he was some Eastern potentate with his dutiful wife following in his wake. Do you ever see the pair of them walking side by side? God forbid they should actually hold hands?'

I suppressed a smile. 'He's just got longer legs. I have exactly the same problem with Graham sometimes.'

Gwen didn't look convinced. 'The man's a misogynist. We've had a meal together a couple of times, and he hardly spoke to me. Only to David. You'd think I wasn't there. He even ignores his own wife. Yesterday at dinner, she tried to ask him something three times. In the end, she had to put a hand on his arm to get his attention. You should have seen the look he gave her.'

'He didn't have a good word to say about Sybil's lectures either,' said David. 'It was quite embarrassing. I'll admit she does have a pedestrian delivery and her slides are pretty basic, but just because she doesn't use all the animation tools that he does is no excuse to rubbish her presentations.'

Gwen became animated. 'You should have seen the look he gave me when I said I thought her explanation of the formation of Iceland and the landscape was good. He said in that patronising tone of his that the job of a cruise lecturer was to entertain not simply to educate.'

The waiter came to collect our empty cups. It was time to leave.

Graham and I exchanged glances as we followed the couple out towards the lifts. If he thought I'd been too harsh in my earlier judgement of the port lecturer when we saw the couple in Nanortalik, at least now he was aware that I was not the only one to take exception to Paul's attitude.


'What do you want to do this afternoon?' Graham asked when we got back to the cabin.

'I haven't really thought about it. What are the options?'

Graham picked up the *Cygnet Daily*. 'The spa is offering a mud foot therapy. Says here it helps to alleviate the discomfort of tired legs. It comes with a pressure point massage!'

I threw a cushion at him.

'I take it that's a no. Killer darts at three o'clock, knock-out table tennis at four-fifteen, or a pop music quiz at five.'

'Find something sensible!'

'How about a film? The theatre is showing a new release in ten minutes. Can't say I've heard of it. It's supposed to be an action comedy about a man who goes looking for his lost dog and gets caught up in a jewellery heist. It's set in Holland.' He raised an eyebrow. 'There'll be popcorn!'

'Okey-dokey. We can always leave if it turns out to be rubbish.'


There were few people in the theatre when we arrived, and we had the pick of the seats. Just before the lights went out, two more people arrived and sat a few rows in front of us.

I recognised Sam and Julie straight away. I felt guilty that I hadn't been to see how they were coping. Three port days on the trot had been enough to keep me busy.

I suppose it was the combination of our conversation about Paul's attitude to women over lunch and seeing the younger couple that prompted the idea. As the opening music accompanying the preamble before the actual film began to play, I found myself mulling over the likelihood of Paul as Doreen's killer. By his own admission, the two had had a pretty fractious encounter in the theatre about their shore excursion in Kirkwall. If she had buttoned-holed him a second time outside the lift when no one else was around, his reaction might not have been quite so restrained. A highly over-exaggerated sense of his own abilities, not to mention male superiority, was one thing, but I had to admit, it was far more likely he'd have cut the combative woman down to size with words rather than physical blows. Besides, what possible motive could he have for stealing Doreen's handbag or ransacking her cabin? What could Doreen have in her possession that he could want so badly?

This was getting me nowhere. I clenched my fists in frustration.

'You okay, love?' Graham whispered.

'Fine.' I settled back down in my seat.

'Popcorn?'

'No thanks.'

He took my hand and threaded my arm through his. I tried to push away all thoughts of Doreen Bowland and concentrated on the film. I can't say I found it riveting. The plot was thin and more or less predictable, the comedy slapstick and somewhat dated but the cinematography – especially the highspeed boat chase through the canals of Amsterdam – did set the heart racing, even if it did go on for longer than it should.

'What did you think of it?' Graham asked when the lights went up.

'I've seen better though I'll admit the scenery was

spectacular.'

'I enjoyed it. Can't say I'd heard of the lead actor before, but he was very good.'

'Hmm. Not bad.'

We'd only just made our way out of the theatre when a voice came over the tannoy, 'Would Mrs Mona Etherington and Mr and Mrs Owen McClean please call the reception desk on 00091 immediately. That's Mrs Mona Etherington and Mr and Mrs McClean please call the reception desk on 00091 immediately.'

'Someone didn't swipe their cruise card when they came back on board,' said Graham as we made our way to the staircase to go back up to our cabin.

'Do you think that's what it is?'

'Bound to be. On-board time was four o'clock and there's always a crush at the top of the stairs when people get off the tenders.'

'I expect you're right.'

Half an hour later, the announcement came again.

'Would Mrs Mona Etherington please call the reception desk immediately on 00091. I repeat, would Mrs Mona Etherington please call the reception desk immediately on 00091.'

'I wonder if that's the Mona I've met. It's not exactly a common name. There can't be that many Monas on board.'

# Chapter 23

'I'll have the Highland game and roast nut terrine followed by the pan-fried haddock with toasted almonds,' I gave my order to the waiter, and handed him my menu.

'Thank you, madam. And for dessert, I can recommend the banana and macadamia nut pudding with maracuja salsa.'

'That does sound good. You've persuaded me.'

'And I'll have that too, plus some extra steamed vegetables with the haddock.'

'Thank you, sir.'

'Heaven knows what maracuja salsa is,' Graham said.

'I think it's a type of passion fruit, but I wouldn't bet on it. We'll have to see when it comes.'

Graham sat back and sipped his wine. 'Have you noticed we're still anchored in the bay? I thought sail away was at five o'clock. Though I don't suppose there's any rush. We've a couple of sea days before we get to Belfast.'

'Goodie. That means we can have a lie-in tomorrow. Three early starts on the trot are getting a bit much for me. Heaven knows why cruising is always portrayed as this leisurely activity with photos of people soaking up the sun and staring out to sea. It's usually all go as far as we're concerned. Even on sea days, there's barely time for a break from one lecture to the next. And we always seem to need at least a week to recover when we get home.'

'You don't have to do everything.'

'True, but why waste the opportunity? We may never

come back to Greenland, and I enjoy the lectures. We do get the odd poor one, but Cygnet have a pretty high standard to keep up. People pay a lot of money, and they expect the best.'

'I take it you don't agree with Paul's estimation of our Dr Sybil Adams?'

'Certainly not. I'll admit I skipped her lecture on the effects of climate change in the Arctic but that was because I didn't fancy the subject. I thought the one she did on Prince Christian Sound was great. She may not be the most dynamic, but she certainly knows her stuff.'

'If you're feeling shattered, do you want an early night?'

'Not particularly. The show cast are doing a new production tonight. The write up in the *Cygnet Daily* sounded rather good. I've forgotten the title, but it has a story theme about a boy who goes to the circus and finds himself pulled into a mystery. Do you fancy it?'

'I'm up for it. The costumes are always spectacular, and the singers are good.'

It was getting on for ten-thirty when we left the theatre.

'That's one of the best shows I've seen. The two dancers doing the trapeze routine were amazing.'

'I agree.' Graham slipped his arm through mine as the crowd pressed together in the narrow corridor due to the sheer number of people ahead waiting to use the lifts. 'The lighting effects were spectacular. It's amazing what they can do with that LED screen covering the back wall.'

We eventually managed to squeeze through to the stairs and back to the cabin.

'Didn't the captain warn us that the seas were going to be a little rough tonight? It doesn't seem too bad to me. Usually when he comes out with something like that it means that it's impossible to walk down the corridors without clinging onto the handrail unless you want to be thrown from side to side.'

'That's true.'

Our cabin steward had closed the curtains when he'd come to tidy the bathroom and turn down the bed. Graham went to the curtain to tweak it aside. 'And there's the reason. We're still at anchor in the fjord. You can see the lights twinkling on the shore.'

'Oh yes. I wonder what the problem is. I hope it's not engine trouble or a mechanical problem of some kind.'

'I doubt it's anything major or the captain would have told us. He did say that the weather was going to get worse tonight and I expect he's delaying our departure to make sure we miss the worst of the storm. Let's hope we don't get woken up in the middle of the night. These modern ships may have reduced the engine noise, but bringing up the anchor makes a hell of a racket.'

# Day 16

At Sea

# Chapter 24

The waitress was at my elbow the moment I'd squeezed myself into the rounded corner of the bench seat.

'What can I get you?'

'I'm expecting a friend. I'll wait till then to order, if that's okay.'

'Of course. I'll come back then.' She gave me a bright smile and placed a small paper doily on the round table in front of me to stop any of the other waiters bothering me.

There were only a few tables occupied and from my vantage point I hoped I'd be able to spot Mona coming in from either entrance. There was a steady stream of people using the Wheelhouse Bar as a cut through from one side of the ship to the other, but after ten minutes there was still no Mona. Perhaps she was running late because she'd overslept. I hadn't had too good a night myself. As Graham had predicted, the prolonged clanking when the anchor was raised in the small hours of the morning had woken me and I had tossed and turned for ages before falling back to sleep. I'd give her five more minutes.

The minutes ticked by. I decided to check round the corner. There was room for a couple more tables and chairs by the window on the port side corridor. I was beginning to get anxious. The announcement for a Mona Etherington to check in last evening for a second time suggested that she had failed to catch the last tender. Had the ship failed to leave because they'd been searching for her ashore?

My heart was pumping. I tried to slow my breathing back

to normal. Graham would tell me I was jumping to conclusions, making all sorts of dramatic scenarios from things that were totally unrelated.

There was one way to find out – check her room. The only problem with that was that I had no idea of her cabin number. My only option was to ask at reception.

'Is it possible for you to give me my friend's cabin number? She lent me her gloves yesterday and I need to return them. Her name is Mona Etherington.' I gave the tall young man behind the desk my most winning smile.

His eyes narrowed and after a moment or two, he said, 'It's not company policy to give out clients' cabin numbers. A matter of security, but if you give me the gloves, I'll make sure they are sent to her cabin.'

'I see. I don't have them with me right now,' I lied. 'I'll drop them down to you later.'

I could tell from his expression he was never going to tell me, and that could only mean one thing. Mona was missing.

'But I've looked everywhere on the ship. I've walked every deck, checked every shop, been round all the lounges twice, tried the card room and the craft room. I even went to the sauna.'

'Perhaps she was in the theatre,' Graham suggested.

I shook my head. 'She told me she never goes to the lectures.'

'Just because you can't find her doesn't mean she's not on the ship. I thought I'd looked all over for you the other day that time when you were just supposed to be collecting the washing. You could easily have missed each other if she moved from one spot to another. Or she could even have been in her cabin.'

I knew Graham was only trying to reassure me, but it wasn't helping. I pushed away my plate of salad and crumbled the rest of my half-eaten roll into pieces.

'You've hardly touched your lunch.'

'Not hungry,' I muttered.

Graham did his best to distract me by talking about the lecture I'd missed. I made what I hoped were all the right noises, but he could have been reciting *The Rime of the Ancient Mariner* for all I knew. Something else had suddenly occurred to me. In all my wanderings, I must have passed by the spot where Richard Jarret habitually sat at least twice. So where was he? Was that more proof that something was up? What did he know about Mona's disappearance?

'Do you mind if I'm a bit late for your lecture this afternoon?'

He looked up from the bed where he was putting all his stuff ready to go down to the theatre. 'I suppose you're going to start looking for Mona again.'

I said nothing. He gave a long sigh.

'If you think it will help. I know you can't stop worrying about her, my darling, but realistically, there is nothing you can do.'

The next half hour passed very slowly as I waited in the cabin for the craft class to begin. There was no point going until everyone had arrived.

'Have you come to join us? The others have already started but I can show you what we're making today.'

'No, sorry. I'm actually looking for a friend.' I looked round the room at the small groups sat round the half dozen tables. Half of the women had their backs to me, but I was reasonably certain she wasn't there. 'She's about 5' 5", shoulder-length fair wavy hair. Sometimes she ties it back in a ponytail.'

'You mean Mona.' Sylvia looked round the room. 'She's one of the regulars but I haven't seen her today. Perhaps she's gone to the lecture this afternoon.'

'I expect you're right. Sorry to have troubled you.'

'No worries.' She turned to one of the crafters who had come up for some help.

I hadn't expected to find Mona but that was my last hope. Now I was stumped for ideas. It was clear from the response I'd received at reception earlier that there was no point in asking any of the ship's staff about her whereabouts. Even if she hadn't made it back to the ship, they wouldn't tell me. The captain and the security officer had done little to disguise their hostility and the only other person who might know was Richard Jarret. He was the only one with who I felt I'd built up some sort of rapport though we hadn't exactly parted on the best of terms at our last meeting. Still there was no harm in trying and what other option did I have?

# Day 17

## At Sea

*Tomorrow we will arrive in Northern Ireland, an area of Great Britain with a long and complicated history.*

*After the Norman Invasion of Ireland, William the Conqueror gave Ulster to John de Coursey whose castles were frequently attacked by Gaelic clans who still held on to the countryside.*

*In 1571, Elizabeth I sent men to put them down for good, and that was followed by nine years of war.*

*When King James I came to the throne, he saw an opportunity to finally take control of the rebellious province. He granted lands and titles to loyal subjects and encouraged an increase in migration from Britain to Ulster, promising work and a new life in what was called the Plantation of Ulster. The largest response was from lowland Scotland and many of the new arrivals to Ulster were Presbyterian protestants.*

*Gaelic clans in Ulster mounted a revolt in 1641, taking advantage of the political turmoil in England during the Civil War.*

*There was a period of peace and prosperity after Charles II was restored to the throne, but it was not to last. The competing forces of James II and William of Orange in Ulster resulted in a death toll of thousands. Things came to a head in 1690 when William sailed to Ireland and marched his troops north to meet James' army at the River Boyne, south of Ulster. William's forces roundly defeated James's troops. After the Battle, James fled to France, never to return.*

*In 1919, the Irish War of Independence broke out which resulted in Ireland being partitioned into Protestant-dominated Northern Ireland*

*and the Catholic-dominated rest of the country in 1921.*
Extract from the Cygnet Daily

# Chapter 25

I'd been awake since around four o'clock. It didn't help trying not to toss and turn so as not to wake Graham. Not that there was much chance of that. He's out like a light as soon as his head hits the pillow and rarely wakes before the alarm. How can men do that? Many of my female friends tell me it's the same with their husbands. Had I been back home, I'd have gone downstairs and read for a bit, but that wasn't an option.

Six-fifteen came and went, I could lie there no longer and crept out of bed. The blackout curtains blocked out all but a chink of light at the edges, enough to be able to grab some fresh underwear and a sweater from the drawer. The wardrobe door creaked ominously as I slid it open, Graham snored and turned over but didn't wake. I pulled out the first pair of trousers I came to but decided not to risk closing the door again.

I decided that the shower was too noisy an option, so after a quick wash, I pulled on my clothes. The check trousers didn't go with my patterned top, but they would have to do for now. My hairbrush was in the drawer under the dressing-table but after combing through my flattened bob with my fingers and patting it into shape, I decided it would pass muster. At this hour, there would be few people about to see me in any case. All I needed now was my cruise card.

Breakfast didn't officially start until seven, but the Ocean Café opened half an hour earlier to serve teas, coffees, and pastries for the early risers. There were still eight minutes to go, but if I took my time climbing up all seven double flights of stairs, they would probably let me in.

At least a dozen people had beaten me to it, including Sam and Julie. It would be rude not to at least go and say hello.

'Another early bird! Is your husband not with you?'

'Graham's still asleep, but I woke early and decided to come and get a cup of tea.'

'If you're on your own, why don't you join us?' Julie pulled out the chair next to her.

'We've got into the habit of coming up first thing. There are fewer people around.'

I frowned. 'You're not still hiding yourselves away?'

'Not really. We even managed to persuade my father to go ashore with us in Greenland. Not in Nuuk obviously, he was still in the infirmary, but we had a wander round Nanortalik for an hour. It was good for him to get off the ship.'

'How is he now?'

'Physically he's fine. Still a bit sore from the fall, but other than that, he's been given a clean bill of health. It's going to take some time for him to adjust to Mum's death, but he's getting there.'

'I don't suppose it helps sitting in his cabin with nothing to take his mind of things.'

'Exactly. That's why we insisted he go ashore if only for a bit of fresh air and a change of scene,' said Sam.

'It was good for him. He was much more like his old self when we got back. He admitted he enjoyed himself. We were going to join one of the tours the next day, but when we realised that even the included tour was classified as strenuous, we decided it might be too much for him,' said Julie.

I nodded. 'It was very hilly and there are no proper paths in the old part of the town. Let's hope you can go ashore when we get to Belfast.'

Sam pursed his lips. 'That might depend on whether that chap Jarret wants to talk to him again today.'

'Why was he asking your father questions?'

'He asked Bill to look round his old cabin to check that nothing had been taken when someone broke in as soon as he came out of the infirmary. Then he started asking all sorts of questions about Doreen and how she'd got on with other passengers,' said Sam.

'I got really cross with him. Told him he had no right to upset Dad. We're all trying to move on from what had happened, not be constantly reminded. He apologised but it didn't stop him from asking again. I wouldn't mind, but he'd already asked both of us soon after Mum died about any unpleasant occurrences, as he put it, that had arisen. Why he wanted to drag it all up again, heaven knows.'

'Perhaps he thought your father might be able to tell him about incidences that happened when you weren't there.'

'But why for goodness' sake? What on earth could that have to do with Mum's death?'

I shrugged my shoulders.

'I told you before. Because he thinks your mother was murdered.'

'Don't be ridiculous, Sam.' Julie slapped her hand on the table.

'Then why was Jarret back again yesterday asking if your mother knew any of the other passengers before the cruise, or if she had struck up a friendship with anyone once she come on board? When we said no, he seemed to think it strange that she had never spent any time talking with anyone else other than the family. Kept going on about it. Asked if she might have struck up a friendship with someone at one of the classes that we might not be aware of. He seemed surprised she never went to any of the activities on board or even went for a coffee by herself.'

Sam gave a mirthless laugh. 'Can you imagine your mum going to an art or craft class? She'd have told the instructor there were doing everything wrong.'

'He even asked if Mum had seen anyone onboard that she knew from before the cruise. He was like a dog with a bone.

Wouldn't let it go. Even asked questions about the people on the trip with us in Kirkwall. Did we remember her talking with anyone?'

'And had she?' I asked.

'Well, there was one woman when we got off the bus at one of the stops. Nice lady. Fair hair, all smiles. But as I told him, I didn't hear what they said to each other, but they weren't arguing, just chatting.'

An ice-cold chill ran down my spine.

'Are you alright?'

'Amanda!'

I suddenly realised they were both looking at me. 'I'm sorry. Miles away. Yes. I'm fine.' I fumbled for the teacup and brought it to my lips.

'Your hand is shaking.'

I took a deep breath and forced myself to take control. 'Forgive me. I was thinking about something else entirely. Please don't think me rude, but I think it's time I went to see if Graham is awake yet. He'll be wondering where I am. I only came up for a quick cup of tea.'

'That was your fault bringing up that stupid theory of yours about them treating Mum's death as murder.' Julie's high-pitched whisper reached me as I went through the archway out into the short stretch of corridor.

I leant back against the wall and closed my eyes. Could it really mean what I thought it did? Could Richard Jarret possibly suspect that Mona had murdered Doreen Bowland? Did that explain why she had failed to return to the ship? Because she knew that Jarret was closing in on her?

But what possible reason could the happy-go-lucky Mona have for killing the objectionable woman? Mona was the type to laugh off any insult. The least likely to get into an argument. Doreen's ability to rub up the wrong way every other person she met was a frequent topic of conversation for the first few days of the cruise. But it was now over a week since there had been any gossip about her. I'd heard nothing to suggest that she and Mona had ever been involved in a fracas.

Had Richard Jarret decided that the two women must have known each other before arriving on the ship? Did Doreen know something about Mona that the friendly, likeable woman might not want made public? Could it be something to do with her first husband? Mona may have claimed that Jack was no criminal, but by all accounts, he mixed with some pretty dodgy characters. Perhaps "Mr Smith" was using the private club to launder money from some nefarious deals or even to distribute drugs.

If Doreen Bowland had recognised Mona and attempted to taunt her about her husband's criminal past, Mona wasn't the type to take it lying down, let alone meekly cave into an attempt at blackmail.

# Chapter 26

It was still dark in the cabin when I eventually got back. Graham was awake. He sat up and switched on the bedside light.

'I thought you were taking a long time in the bathroom. I didn't realise you'd gone out.'

'You were still dead to the world, and I was dying for a cup of tea.'

'Why didn't you make one in the room? You said last night you were looking forward to having tea in bed as we didn't have to make an early start.'

'I didn't want to disturb you.'

He threw back the covers, climbed out of bed and went to open the curtains. A deep frown furrowed his brow when he turned to face me.

'You look upset. Has something happened?'

I told him the whole sorry story.

He took my hands and pulled me down to sit next to him on the bed.

'It's a bit of a leap to think that Mona is a suspect in that woman's death.'

'Why else would Jarret ask if she and Doreen had ever been in an argument?'

'That you would have to ask him.'

'I've a good mind to.' He took a quick intake of breath, but before he could say anything, I continued, 'Don't worry. I'm not going to. I just wish I knew what's happened to her.'

'We don't even know for certain that she isn't on the ship.

All this speculation based on only a handful of assumptions isn't going to get you anywhere. I know you're worried about your friend, but, right now, there is nothing you can do, so let me get showered and dressed and we'll go and get some breakfast. I take it you haven't eaten yet?'

I shook my head.

The morning's lecture was another port talk. We'd been to Belfast a couple of times before, but Paul's lectures were always interesting, and though we hadn't yet been told which shore excursions we would be escorting, it was always good to know as much as possible about the tours on offer.

When the lecture had finished and the theatre had begun to empty, Graham said, 'Do you mind if we hang back for a bit? There's something I'd like to ask Paul.'

'No problem.'

There was the usual handful of people eager to ask questions at the end of most lectures, so we took our time strolling down to the front.

'Great lecture, Paul.'

'Glad you liked it.'

'I particularly liked how you focused in on the bronze statues at the base of the Queen Victoria monument outside the town hall and zoomed in so we could see the detail. I'd love to know how you do that.'

'It's not that difficult. I'll show you if you like.'

'That would be great.'

'How about now? Let's see if we can find a table somewhere. Do you want to get your laptop, and you can have a go yourself?'

Graham turned to me. 'You don't mind, do you?'

'Of course not. Take your time. I'll see you back in the cabin later.'

The two men were obviously going to be occupied for some time. There was no point in me sitting in the cabin twiddling my thumbs, so I decided to go down to reception and collected a copy of the day's newspaper and a sudoku.

I found a comfortable chair in the window opposite and sat down to read.

The news from back home was nothing we hadn't already learnt. Britain was still sweltering under the exceptional heatwave and the prolonged lack of rain meant that reservoirs were low. Two more water authorities had banned the use of hosepipes and there were more dire warnings about the effects on farming and threats of shortages and high prices. I skipped the Yesterday in Parliament section. Our elected leaders continued to behave no better than squabbling kids in the playground. The world news on page two was no more uplifting and I never bother with the sports pages. I threw it onto the table in disgust.

I didn't have a pen with me which meant I couldn't attempt the sudoku. The last thing I wanted was to be left alone with my thoughts. Graham was right. All the worrying in the world wasn't going to solve what had led to Doreen's death or help to find Mona. I headed for the stairs.

Ahead of me in the corridor was a waiter carrying a small tray. He knocked on a door halfway down and waited for a response. He had left the door wide open and, as I approached, I could hear them talking. I recognised the occupant's voice.

I closed the intervening distance in four long strides and took a step inside the room.

'Mona had nothing to do with what happened to Doreen!' Even to my own ears, my plaintive cry sounded hysterical.

Richard Jarret looked up from his desk in surprise. The waiter gave me a terrified glance, danced round me and beat a hasty exit.

Jarret and I stared at each other for what seemed an age, before he said calmly, 'Push the door to and come and sit down.'

'I'm sorry. I didn't mean to burst in like that,' I mumbled as I slid onto the chair opposite him. Feeling suddenly bolder, I said defensively, 'But I know you're wrong. Why would Mona have any reason to kill that woman? I know her. She wouldn't hurt anyone. Mona is a confident outgoing sort who couldn't care less what anyone thinks of her and her lifestyle. Certainly not the type to let the likes of someone like Doreen provoke her.'

'Whoa.' He put up his hands warding me off. 'Why would you think that I consider Mona to be a suspect?'

'Why else would you have asked Julie and Sam more questions about who Doreen might have an altercation with, the moment Mona goes missing?'

'Mrs Mitchell, you have been told several times not to discuss Mrs Bowland's death with anyone and I personally asked you not to…'

'And I haven't!' Losing my temper now would defeat the object. I needed him on my side, to see my point of view. 'People talk to *me*. I ran into Julie and Sam at breakfast. I assure you I did not bring up the subject. They told me about your visit yesterday and what you had asked about. I made no comment. In actual fact, I made my excuses and left.'

He looked at me long and hard before he said, 'Very well.'

'Before you tell me to forget all about Doreen's death, I'd like nothing better, believe me, but I can't. I'm the one who found her body. For some reason I can't explain, I feel I owe it to her to find out how she died. Everything that has happened since convinces me she was murdered. How else do you explain the arrival of a policeman at the next port to conduct an investigation?' He opened his mouth to protest, but I rushed on, 'That night, there was a forensic investigation of the carpets outside the lifts, which indicates that at the very least you suspected that the body had been moved. Why would anyone move a body unless it was dead or dying? The stolen handbag and the search of her room only confirm that she had something that someone was prepared to kill for. I assure you, I'm not trying to play private detective. I wouldn't know how, and I don't have the means. It's just that I don't want to

leave this ship without answers. I've kept my part of the

bargain. I've kept schtum. Apart from Graham, no one knows I was the one who found Doreen's body or anything else I've discovered along the way. I feel in return I'm owed the truth but so far everyone keeps fobbing me off.'

He sat back in his chair. The silence hung in the air.

'My, my. That was some speech.'

'And can you deny anything that I've said?'

'Let's assume for the moment, although it cannot be confirmed until a pathologist can conduct a post-mortem when we return to Britain, that Mrs Bowland was murdered. Has it occurred to you that you yourself must be one of the most likely suspects. You claim to have discovered the body and you have made it your mission to attempt to discover what the official investigation has so far uncovered.'

'But that's ridiculous. I never even spoke to the woman in passing never mind had a conversation.'

'We only have your word for that.'

'But how could I have taken Doreen's handbag without being seen? I went into the dining- room with Graham and two other people, and I never left my seat until all four of us left together after the meal. As for breaking into her cabin, how did I manage to get hold of a keycard? There's no way I could have done it.'

He had his elbows on the table with his hands covering the lower half of his face, but I could see his shoulders gently heaving.

'Very funny,' I snapped.

'Yes. I'd worked that out too.'

'But you considered it?'

'Naturally. That's my job.'

'So you are a policeman,' I said triumphantly.

'Touché.'

'It's good to know that what happened to Doreen isn't just being swept under the carpet.'

'I can assure you her death is being fully investigated.'

'Then I'll leave it all in your capable hands.' I smiled and got to my feet. At the door, I turned and back to say, 'Thank you, Inspector.'

As I pulled the door closed behind me, I heard a muttered, '*Chief* inspector.'

The corridor was empty which meant that there was no one to witness the crazy old woman giggling like a schoolgirl as she skipped down the corridor.

# Chapter 27

The door banged against the wall as Graham burst into the cabin, a self-satisfied smirk on his face.

'That was a really worthwhile session.'

'It certainly took you long enough,' I joked.

'Paul showed me just how to use the zoom and wheel animations and helped me enhance three or four of my slides for this afternoon's lecture. It's amazing how simple they are but very effective. I had no idea it was possible to do it at all, never mind how to do it.'

He insisted on showing me the changes he'd made there and then.

Half an hour later, he was still investigating other animation tools. 'I wonder what effect the grow and shrink would have on this slide.'

'If you want to have any lunch, I suggest you leave that till later. If we don't go up to the Ocean Café soon, you are going to be late for your lecture this afternoon.'

'Is that the time already? How time flies when you're having fun.'

It was relatively busy upstairs.

'There are a couple of empty tables down at the far end. You get yourself a salad while I go and grab a couple of seats.'

Salad may well be my lunchtime staple, but the smell of vinegar took me to the hot counter where I could see someone liberally dousing their plate piled high with chips.

Fish and chips! What could be better?

Graham looked up in surprise when he saw my plate. 'Chips at lunchtime!'

'I'm hungry.'

'It's great to see you've got your appetite back. You've barely eaten enough to keep a mouse alive these last few days. You're looking pretty pleased with yourself. Did you have a good morning?'

I wasn't sure if I should tell him about bearding Richard Jarret in his den or that I'd discovered that I'd been right all along and his man from head office was a policeman – a chief inspector, no less. Perhaps it was something I shouldn't even share with Graham. True I hadn't specifically said it, but I had implied to DCI Jarret that I would not reveal his real identity to anyone.

'I went for a coffee and then got chatting, as you do.'

He pushed away his empty plate and dabbed his lips with the napkin. 'That was tasty.'

'I'm not going to have a dessert, so don't wait for me.'

'Okay. If you're sure.' He scraped back the chair and merged into the melee heading for the buffet counters leaving me to relish my last few mouthfuls.

He returned with a warmed brownie covered in a thick chocolate sauce.

'That's not fair! To do two of my favourites at lunchtime ought not to be allowed.'

'I brought two spoons, but if you want to get your own, I'll have no problem polishing this off by myself.' He dangled the second spoon between us.

I swiped it before he could seize it back. 'Just a taste.'

The rich aroma hit my nostrils before the silky-smooth warm chocolate rolled over my taste buds. I closed my eyes to savour every moment. The texture of the confection was just right – crisp and crunchie but moist enough to melt in the mouth without being soggy. I licked the spoon to ensure I consumed every morsel. It took every inch of willpower I possessed to put down the spoon.

'I'll get us a coffee.' I jumped to my feet. There was no way I could sit watching him eat the rest.

We took our time over coffee and eventually strolled hand in hand back to the cabin in time for Graham to change into a suit, collect his laptop and head to the theatre for his lecture.

There were already a few people dotted about the auditorium. The technician appeared from the projection box carrying a head mike, and while he and Graham were busy up on stage connecting up the laptop and all the rest of the palaver, I went to get Graham a glass of water.

The theatre gradually began to fill up over the next twenty minutes. David and Gwen came down to wish Graham good luck. It was as we were all chatting that Kirsten arrived to introduce the lecture.

'I'm glad I've caught all four of you. Friday night I'm arranging a thank you dinner for all the guest speakers and instructors. I decided not to make it the last night as you'd all be busy packing. It'll be in the Italian restaurant at seven, if that's alright.'

'That would be great. Amanda and I have never been in either of the speciality restaurants.' Both Mario's, the Italian restaurant, and The Pagoda House, the Far Eastern restaurant had a booking system and priority was always given to the other passengers. We were not prohibited from dining in either restaurant, but it meant that we had to turn up on spec to see if there were any available tables.

'That's what I thought, which is why I thought it might be a special treat. At this stage of the cruise, passengers will have had a chance to try them both so there won't be any pressure on tables. I will be sending an email round to everyone, but I thought I'd give you both a heads up.'

'Looking forward to it,' said David.

Kirsten glanced at her watch. 'Right, if you're ready, Mr Mitchell, we're up!'

The cruise director switched on her hand-held

microphone and mounted the stairs with Graham in her wake and the rest of us sat down on the front row.

It was one of the best presentations that Graham had ever given. True, his newly amended slides were impressive, but his whole performance was relaxed, assured and engaging. His confidence was on a high. Whether that was down to his newfound skill, a good meal or the promise of another as an acknowledgement that his skills were appreciated by management, or possibly a combination of all three, he had his audience eating out of his hand. The applause at the end went on for some time and when he came down the steps from the stage, he was surrounded by people coming to congratulate him. They were still there when Sybil arrived to set up her lecture.

Outside the theatre, Graham said, 'I want to hear Sybil's lecture, but I need to drop my laptop back in the cabin and change out of my suit.'

I glanced at my watch. 'No rush. We've got just under half an hour before it starts. I'll come back with you, and we can come back down together.'

At five-thirty, we went to collect our escort rucksacks for the next day's excursions from behind reception.

Graham handed me the one with my name on it then pulled out the clipboard with all the paperwork from his own. 'Looks like I'm on 'The Legendary Giant's Causeway'. What are you doing?'

'Mine's 'Scenic Coast and Glens'. I wouldn't swear to it, but I thought I'd opted for the trip to Hillsborough Castle. That was only a three- or four-hour trip. The glens excursion is virtually all day.'

'Hi, you two.' Liam, the young excursions manager had come in from behind us. Despite his name, his black hair, dark brown eyes and vaguely coffee coloured skin owed more to a hint of Indian or Pakistani origins than Irish. 'Didn't mean to make you jump, Amanda. The

Hillsborough trip had to be cancelled at the last minute. I tried to catch you earlier to ask if you'd be happy to do the Scenic Coast and Glens excursion instead. Will it be a problem? It's a lovely drive and the waterfalls at Glenariff are spectacular.'

'It's not a problem. Graham is going to be out all day too so it's no big deal.'

'Thanks. I appreciate that. They are going to be the last excursions for this trip, so enjoy.'

'I'm sure we will. Does that mean that after tomorrow, you have a couple of days off before we get back to Southampton?'

'If only!' He pulled a face. 'I've got all the tours to get sorted for the next cruise. You wouldn't believe all the stuff we still need to finalise. There are two port agents I can't get hold of to check how many coaches are available, and another one is having problems sourcing sufficient guides. It's always the same. Life at sea is a constant lurch from one mini crisis to the next. Anyway, have a good evening the pair of you. I'll see you tomorrow.'

'And you,' we both chorused to his rapidly retreating back as he disappeared into the bowels of the ship.

We shared our table at dinner with a pleasant, friendly couple from the Yorkshire Dales. Stan, a stocky, rugged, florid-faced man was clearly an out-door type, and it was no surprise to learn that he was a retired farmer.

'Retired in name only,' said his wife Elsie, raising her eyes to the ceiling. 'He's back at the farm at least a couple of days a week.'

'I help out when they're busy. They need all the help they can get come lambing. It's hard for our Tom. It was bad enough in my day, but more and more hill farmers are having to sell up. If it weren't for the bed and breakfast business our daughter-in-law's been building up these last eight years, they'd have gone under.'

'There are some wonderful walks in the area, and they get

a lot of bird watchers too,' said Elsie.

'I don't think we've ever been to the Dales. We had a few days in York many years ago when our two were children. Funnily enough, only last week we were talking about getting away into the countryside for a few days and the Dales was high on the list of options. These last few years, we've spent all our holidays abroad. Britain has some attractive areas that we've never ever seen,' I said.

'We have some of the most beautiful countryside in the whole of England, and very pretty, unspoilt villages. Grassington has become quite famous in the last couple of years ever since they started filming *All Creatures Great and Small*. It's the fictional Darrowby where the Siegfried Farnon and James Herriot have their veterinary practice. Our farm is only ten miles away. It's given a tremendous boost to the B&B.'

'It sounds perfect for a mini break. You must give us the details. Do you have a business card?' said Graham.

'I didn't think to bring any, but I can give you their web address,' said Stan.

'Grassington is well worth a visit. It's a small market town with a central cobbled square and an old pump pouring water into a bucket. The shops all have the original fronts and there's a historic inn, the Devonshire. When they're filming, it gets transformed into the Drovers Arms where Tristan does much of his drinking. Another historic building is the Congregational Church, that's over two hundred years old. There's also a folk museum and the information centre for the National Park. And of course, it has lots of good places to eat.'

Elsie gave us lots more suggestions of the nearby places we might like to see, and we both felt enthused by the idea of a visit by the time we'd finished our meal. Not that it was the only topic of conversation which ranged over a variety of subjects including their enjoyment of the cruise and all the ship had to offer.

Our table was one of the last to leave. As we made our

way back to the cabin, Graham said, 'They were an interesting couple. Full of energy. They both did the Signal Hill hike in Narsarsuaq and the hike round the Great Lake in Qaqortoq. Not bad going for a couple in their eighties.'

'Obviously working on a hill farm keeps you fit.'

We were too late to see the show in the theatre. Not that either of us were bothered as a male vocalist singing songs from Frank Sinatra and the Rat Pack wasn't really to our taste in any case. The alternative entertainment was either dancing to the music of the Sea Dream Band in the Ocean Lounge or a quiz in the Wheelhouse Bar.

Graham propped up his pillow and sat on the bed clicking through the in-cabin entertainment options. 'Fancy watching a film?'

'As long as it doesn't go on too long. We've an early start tomorrow.'

'How about a documentary? There are some interesting ones on the National Geographic channel.'

'Fine. You choose while I just take a quick look at the itinerary for the excursion I'm going to be escorting.'

As I was reading the details, my thoughts drifted back to the tour I'd shared with Mona. It suddenly struck me. I'd burst into DCI Jarret's office fully intending to find out about what had happened to Mona, and that was the one thing I hadn't asked.

# Day 18

*Belfast, Northern Ireland*

*Belfast is the capital and largest city in Northern Ireland though it is relatively small with a population of around 480,000.*

*Although a castle was built here in Norman times, it was only after Sir Arthur Chichester was made Lord Deputy of Ireland by James I, that Belfast grew to prominence. The start of the seventeenth century saw an influx of French Protestants fleeing religious persecution in their own country. They introduced linen weaving to Belfast and the city prospered on the growing linen industry. Belfast became the fastest growing industrial city in the whole of Britain. Industry flourished with rope making, cotton spinning and in 1862 the Harland & Wolff shipyard was founded and became one of the world's largest shipbuilders. The company built the majority of the ocean liners for the White Star Line, including the ill-fated RMS Titanic.*

*Queen Victoria granted Belfast, city status in 1888 and this was the time of Belfast's 'Golden Age' when most of its great buildings were constructed, including the City Hall, the Grand Opera House and Queen's University.*

*In the late 20th century, Belfast suffered from high unemployment. The old industries of linen, engineering, and shipbuilding declined, and many workers were laid off. Discontent grew, which led to The Troubles that lasted for 30 years.*

*The Troubles have left their mark, but today Belfast's historic buildings and places of interest make this beautiful city a Mecca for tourists.*

Extract from the Cygnet Daily

# Chapter 28

Our guide for the day introduced himself as Sean. He was a small wiry man with short-cropped mousy hair flecked with grey. We chatted as we stood by the coach waiting for the group to arrive.

'Here they come now,' said Sean in his attractive Irish lilt.

As the passengers handed over their tickets and boarded the coach, I noticed one man hanging back looking over his shoulder, a slight frown on his face. He still appeared reluctant to climb the steps even when everyone else was on board.

'Are you waiting for someone?' I asked.

He shook his head. 'Not really. I did say I'd join up with someone after we did a previous outing together, but it wasn't a firm arrangement.'

'Is your name Alastair by any chance?'

He spun his head to look straight at me. 'How on earth did you know that?'

'I'm a friend of Mona's.'

There was no time to continue our conversation as we were holding up the departure of the coach which was on a tight schedule. I took my place at the back of the coach and before long we were heading out of the port and driving north along the coast road.

The sun was shining, showing off the majestic cliffs and stunning views across the Irish Sea to best advantage, but my thoughts were elsewhere. As we passed through the little port of Larne, I caught only the gist of Sean's explanation of the origin of the town's name which had something to do with the son of an ancient Irish king.

'Coming up soon is Ballygally and if you look to the left, you'll see Ballygally Castle. It dates back to 1625 when it was built by James Shaw from Scotland. Today, it's a hotel. But be warned, if you ever come back and decide to stay there, it's not for the faint-hearted. It has more ghosts than guests.'

Preoccupied with my own thoughts though I was, even I found myself laughing at the pained expression on Sean's face as he told his tale.

'The most famous ghost is James' sixteen-year-old wife, Lady Isabella Shaw. James had a dark, cruel streak and she quickly learnt that the only reason he'd married her was to produce an heir. When she gave birth to a daughter, he was so angry he dragged the child from her and had Isabella locked up in the turret room at the top of the castle tower. On a cold December night, she climbed onto the windowsill, opened the window and threw herself from the battlements. If you look carefully up at the tiny window, you may just catch sight of her white wedding dress stained with blood.'

'Can we stop to take a photo?' someone called out.

The request was echoed throughout the coach.

Sean consulted with the driver. 'We're not supposed to stop, but if you're all very quick Paddy will find somewhere to pull off. Just five minutes mind. No longer.'

It wasn't long enough to have a proper talk with Alastair, but I could at least suggest we have a chat at the next stopping point. On second thoughts, that might put him on his guard. Best to wait and make my approach seem more casual.

The opportunity arose at the Glenariff Forest Park after we had all climbed back up the side of the gorge and settled ourselves in the Glenariff Tea House for a well-deserved cup of tea and scones.

As always, I was the last to arrive with the stragglers. The area set aside for the Sea Dream guests was crowded and it took a moment or two before I spotted Alastair and as luck would have it, there was an empty chair next to him. I recognised several faces around the table most of whom were already busy ladling jam and cream onto their plates. Some, including Alastair, had also been served tea. Gentleman that he was, he leant forward, lifted the plate of scones and held it for me to take one.

'Thank you.'

One of the waitresses arrived carrying a large pot. 'Coffee, madam?'

'I'd prefer tea, please.'

She beckoned to one of the other servers.

'I think I need this. It was quite a climb, but well worth it.'

Nods and murmurs of agreement were given around the table before everyone resumed their conversation with the person sitting next to them.

I turned to Alastair. 'Did you get any good photos?'

'I hope so, but it was impossible to stand far enough back to get in the whole width of the falls.'

'It is tricky with all those trees and overhanging branches.'

He turned his head to look directly at me. 'You're Graham Mitchell's wife, aren't you?'

'That's right.'

'I thought I recognised you. I've seen you with him at the front of the theatre when he gives his lectures. Which are very good by the way. I really enjoyed the one he gave yesterday on the Vikings in Ireland. That was his best. I had no idea that they founded Dublin and established it as their most important slave market.'

The small talk continued for some time. I'd almost decided that it was going to be down to me to bring up the subject of Mona when he said, 'When we were getting on the coach, you said something about being a friend of Mona's.'

'I've met her around the ship, and a couple of times we've been on a tour together. She says it's much more fun with someone else. She mentioned that she teamed up with an Alastair in Nanortalik and I wondered if that might be you.'

He smiled. 'That's right. We made tentative plans for today as well, but perhaps she was booked on the coach that was leaving later.'

'I expect that's it. I haven't seen her for a few days, so I don't know her plans.'

'No, I haven't seen her either. We don't tend to cross each other's path on sea days. I usually spend most of the day in the theatre, but Mona's not really interested in any of the lectures. She's much more of an active person. Never misses the ballroom and line dance lessons.'

'She is quite a bundle of energy, isn't she? I know she's a widow, but I can't remember if she has any children.'

'A stepson in Australia somewhere, but none of her own. Her only blood relative is a sister up in Hartlepool, I believe. I don't think they're that close, just a letter at Christmas and a birthday card. That's the problem when families live so far apart isn't it? You mean to keep in touch but the months flash past.'

'Too true.'

# Chapter 29

My tour was back on the ship long before Graham's was due to return. After all the morning's exercise, I was ravenous. All I'd eaten that day was a bowl of berries and a slice of toast at breakfast plus a scone and a small slice of fruit cake in the Glenariff Tea Rooms. Officially, they stopped serving lunch in the Ocean Café at two o'clock, but I was hoping that today they may have extended it a little because of the tours returning that much later. It was worth a try.

Finding out what had happened to Mona was still a priority. The only person who might know and might just be persuaded to tell me was DCI Jarret, but that would have to wait. I threw my rucksack on the bed, shrugged out of my anorak, changed out of my boots, and headed for the stairs.

The port side of the Ocean Café had been closed but an arrow in the entrance pointed me to the other side. Few of the tables were occupied and the waiters had already begun laying up for dinner at the far end.

'The hot counter will be closing in ten minutes,' said a voice at my elbow.

I smiled at the white-clad kitchen hand replenishing the depleted pile of plates below the counter. 'Thanks, but I'm going to stick to my salad.'

Working my way along the various options on the salad bar, I selected tuna then added mixed lettuce leaves, sliced tomato, cucumber, radish, grated carrot, and beetroot. I inspected the range of potato salad, coleslaw and pastas bathed in creamy calorific sauces but decided to stick to my earlier resolution. By the time I'd reached the selection of dressings at the far end of the counter, a stream of latecomers began to arrive. Most of them had been on the Scenic Coasts and Glens tour with me. Some must have come straight up as they were still in their outdoor coats which they were now busy removing and hanging on the backs of their chairs.

I looked around to see if I could spot Alastair before finding a table by the window in a quiet corner. Not that it mattered. There was probably nothing more that he could tell me about Mona. I was still convinced that her disappearance had nothing to do with her being responsible for Doreen Bowland's death, but a nagging voice at the back of my mind kept telling me that if Doreen's murderer was worried that the police were fast closing in, it made sense to use the opportunity to leave the ship. The only person who was missing, at least as far as I knew, was Mona. DCI Jarret had never actually said that he didn't consider her a suspect. Thinking back to our conversation, he had very cleverly steered me away from Mona's possible involvement by suggesting I might well be at the top of the suspect list.

I may have concocted a wild theory about a previous connection between Doreen and Mona, but that's all it was – a fanciful idea with no basis in fact except in my overactive imagination. I had no proof that the two women had ever met. Neither Sam nor Julie had given any indication of their hometown. Now that was a question I could legitimately find the answer to. It might be a trifle more difficult to find out if Doreen had ever been to Brighton on holiday or a day trip, but there was no harm in trying if only to reassure myself Mona had to be innocent of Doreen's murder. Julie had mentioned that they'd been hoping to take her father ashore in Belfast, but I had no idea if the family were on a tour or were planning to catch the shuttle bus into the centre.

I finished the last of my coffee and decided to take the long way back to the cabin passing through the public areas. The area around the pool was virtually deserted with only a few people at the poolside tables who had decided to eat lunch outside. There was no sign of either Sam or Julie in the Ocean Lounge at the far end of the top deck, the Wheelhouse Bar, or the library which was on the same deck as our cabin. DCI Jarret's favourite chair looking down onto the main deck below was also empty. Not that I'd expected him to be there. I peered over the balcony into the Atrium Lounge below, but the view was very limited. The only way to be sure the couple weren't there, was go down myself and check. Tidying the cabin and filling in all the post-excursion forms could wait.

My wanderings took me past DCI Jarret's office. Tempting though it was to knock and see if I could persuade him to tell me what he knew about Mona's disappearance, it was probably best to give some thought as to how to phrase my questions.

It was almost five o'clock before Graham was back.

'I was beginning to give up on you. I expected you back an hour ago.'

He raised his eyes heavenward, dumped his stuff on the bed and let out a long sigh.

'As bad as that, eh? What happened?'

'One of my lot went climbing on the rocks, slipped and dislocated a finger. Luckily the medics arrived pretty quickly and sorted him out, but we all had to wait around until he'd been treated and was ready to come with us. The guide phoned the restaurant and told them we were going to be a bit late for lunch. They were none too happy, but at least they were able to accommodate us.'

'So you did at least get fed.'

'True, but it wasn't exactly the best meal I've ever had. The meat was over-cooked, and the vegetables were all soggy because they'd been kept warm for so long.'

'So how is the poor invalid?'

'I've just taken him down to the medical centre for an x-ray. To be honest, I had more problems keeping his wife from having hysterics. Henry didn't make any fuss at all.'

'A dislocated finger isn't like putting out a shoulder. It's not nearly as painful for one thing. Here, let me take your jacket and I'll hang it up for you. I suppose you've got an accident report to write up now?'

'I've filled in the essentials. His name and cabin number and how it all happened. I did that while we were waiting at the information centre at the Giant's Causeway. I've just got the second page to do, but first let's go and get a cup of tea and you can tell me all about your trip.'

# Chapter 30

Graham had had enough on his plate without me going on about my worries. He'd been there for me enough times on this cruise, and it was only right that I supported him now. Not that I didn't take the opportunity to look around for Sam and Julie as we sought out somewhere comfortable to sit in the Atrium Lounge. The tension visibly eased from Graham's shoulders as he sat back in the armchair taking the occasional sip from the cup he was cradling in his hands as he listened to me prattling on about the wonderful scenery on my morning's excursion.

'Fancy some more tea?' I said as I lifted the lid off the pot and peered inside. 'There's enough for at least another half cup each.'

'No. I'm fine. You have it.'

He leant forward and replaced his cup on the saucer. 'I'll go up and fill in the rest of the accident form while you drink it. I take it you've already done all your paperwork?'

'I filled in all the forms while I was waiting for you, and I've already handed everything back to Liam.'

He gave a long sigh. 'That's something else I need to do. Liam wasn't around when I got back to the ship. I need to go and tell him about the accident. He won't be best pleased if he knows nothing about it when someone starts asking questions. Looks like I might be a while, so no rush – take your time drinking your tea.'

'Will do. See you back in the cabin.'

Once Graham had left, I felt restless. Leaving my second

cup of tea to go cold, I was on my feet. I made a slow circle around the lounge just to check that none of the Bowland family were on the far side of the central serving counter. Not that I really expected to see them. My route eventually took me past DCI Jarret's office.

I found myself giving a gentle tap on the door before I'd even worked out what to say.

'Come in.'

I put my head round the door. 'It's me.'

'So I see.' The intelligent eyes were wary.

'Do you have a moment?' Without waiting for an answer, I stepped inside, closed the door and leant back against it. 'I promise I won't keep you. It's only that I'm worried about Mona. I know she failed to get back onto the ship when we left Greenland, and I wondered if you knew what had happened to her. There's no one else I can ask.'

The silence seemed to hang as we locked eyes across the length of the narrow windowless room.

'You mentioned that you knew her. Was that before you came on the ship?'

'No. We'd been on a couple of tours together and struck up a friendship. She's a fun lady.'

'What exactly do you mean by that?'

'Outgoing. An extrovert. A bit of a free spirit. She likes dancing. From what she said, she went up to the late-night party most evenings.'

He smiled. 'A bit of a raver, eh?'

I wasn't sure what he was implying. 'She liked a drink certainly, and from the way she dressed and behaved, she could have been taken for a woman a good ten, fifteen years younger than she was, but I doubt she was out at a nightclub every night back home.'

'Point taken. I didn't take you for one of the late-night crowd.'

'I'm not.'

'So how come the two of you became so friendly?'

'As I said, she was on the walking tour in Nuuk that I was

escorting and then again in the same tiny fishing boat when we went to see the snout of the glacier in the next port. We've chatted when we've seen each other around the ship. Then in Qaqortoq, we sat next to each other in the tender. I'd forgotten my gloves and she lent me her spare pair. We were on different tours, so I didn't see her again. The two of us were supposed to meet up for coffee the next day so that I could return them, but she never turned up. I've looked all over for her. I'm worried about her. She didn't like wandering round on her own even when there was free time on a tour. She was nervous of getting lost and being left behind when the ship left port. That's why she preferred to team up with someone. She was on her own that day, and because it was a morning tour, I'm convinced she would have come straight back to the ship and not stayed ashore.'

'Did she talk about her past? What can you tell me about her?'

I told him about her being a singer and moving with her husband to Brighton and the *Albion Club,* but I kept back what Mona had told me about the underworld connection. I was sure it wasn't relevant and mentioning it would only confuse matters.

'I see.' He frowned looking thoughtful.

'She never came back on the ship, did she?' He didn't answer. 'Do you have any news?'

'Let me reassure you, Mrs Etherington has been found.'

The tension eased from my shoulders. It wasn't until then that I was aware that I'd been holding my breath.

'Thank goodness. That is a relief.'

He smiled, picked up his pen and looked back down at the papers on his desk. Clearly, I was dismissed.

'But how is she going to get back? She will have left her passport in her cabin. And besides that, Greenland doesn't have an international airport…'

He put up a hand to stop me. 'The Cruise company will handle all that. Arrangements have already been made. Now, if that is all, I am very busy.'

179

There was clearly something he wasn't telling me. He was choosing his words too carefully.

'Something's happened. Has she been arrested?'

His puzzled frown seemed quite genuine. 'No. Why would you think that?'

When I didn't answer, he said, 'Is this to do with the death of Doreen Bowland? To my knowledge, Mona Etherington had no association with her at all. Unless you can tell me something different.'

I slowly shook my head. 'Mona's dead, isn't she?'

He gave a long sigh, waved me to a chair, and said in a quiet voice, 'Come and sit down.'

I'm not quite sure what happened next. I found myself sitting with a cut-glass tumbler in my hand with an inch of brandy in the bottom.

'I don't drink spirits.'

'It's medicinal.' He knelt down on one knee and gently lifted the glass to my lips. The fumes alone made me choke, but once the fiery liquid had warmed the ice core that had formed in my stomach, I pulled myself together.

'What happened?'

'We don't know yet.'

'Was it an accident?'

'We don't have the details yet.'

The slight pause before his answer confirmed my gut feeling. It couldn't possibly have been a traffic accident. I hadn't seen a single moving vehicle the whole time I'd been ashore. It's why all the excursions were graded as difficult. Walking was the only option. Apart from the central square and the harbour, the town was built on steep hillsides. And Mona wasn't the type to go off climbing up slopes on her own.

'But why would anyone want to kill her?'

'As yet, we do not have the details as to how she met her death. The Greenland authorities are still conducting enquiries.' The official-speak didn't fool me for a moment.

'You must have some idea. If it wasn't robbery, then it has

to have something to do with the murder of Doreen Bowland.'

He stood up and pulled a chair alongside mine and there was no hint of sarcasm in his voice when he asked, 'What makes you think the two are connected? Do you have any evidence?'

I shook my head, handed back the almost empty glass and looked down at my hands in my lap.

'You appear to have had more to do with Mona Etherington than anyone else. Is there anything you are aware of that links her to what happened to Doreen Bowland?'

'As far as I know, the two never ran into one another,' I mumbled.

'You don't sound too sure about that.'

He'd been honest with me, perhaps it was time to tell him about Jack and his dubious connections.

'But Mona swore her husband wasn't a criminal.'

'Do you know Jack's surname?'

I shook my head. 'But he owned the *Albion Club* in Brighton. I don't know if that helps.'

He nodded. 'We don't seem to have much background on Mrs Etherington at all. Not even a next of kin.'

'I believe there's a sister in Halifax, but I don't think they were close.' I took a tissue from my pocket and blew my nose. I still felt pretty shaky. 'I don't understand, why would anyone want to murder her?'

He gave a long sigh. 'I really don't know. Unless she saw something.'

'If it was to do with Doreen's murder and the killer was frightened, she would say something, why would he wait for almost two weeks before killing her?'

'Could Mona have been blackmailing him?'

My whole body bristled with indignation. 'No!'

He stared at me calmly. 'Can you think of an alternative explanation?'

Much as I hated to admit it, it would have been wrong for

the DCI not to have considered it, and I had no way to disprove his suggestion. I reminded myself that earlier, even I had wondered if Mona had been Doreen's murderer and used the opportunity to evade capture by leaving the ship.

'Did Mona take her passport with her?'

He looked a little surprised at my question. 'No. It was in the safe in her cabin. Why do you ask?'

I shrugged, but at least it scuppered my theory. I didn't know if I was pleased about that or not. Mona as a blackmailer was no more an attractive proposition than as a murderer.

'Mrs Mitchell. Amanda. I'm aware that people talk to you. They appear to tell you things, impart confidences about matters that they would never discuss with me. Are you aware of anything, no matter how small or insignificant that might help in my investigation?'

'I don't think so. Nothing that you don't know already. Doreen seems to have upset everyone she came across and had a very public shouting match with her son-in-law in the Atrium Lounge, but nothing that would lead to anyone killing her. It is possible I suppose that an argument became so heated that someone lashed out. Presumably her death was not premeditated. The killer must have ended up covered in blood when he dragged the body into the lift thus running the risk of being seen fleeing back to his cabin. But that wouldn't account for the stolen handbag and the break-in. The most logical explanation is that she had something he wanted which she refused to give him.'

'Any ideas as to what that might be?'

'None at all. As I said before, it had to be small to fit into a handbag. Something that would incriminate him. A document of some sort perhaps. I'll think it over. If I get any ideas, I'll get back to you.'

I got to my feet and turned to leave.

Before I'd taken more than a couple of steps, he said, 'Amanda. The last thing I want is for you to start asking questions. May I remind you, there is a killer out there. I already have two murders on my hands, the last thing I want is a third.'

My first instinct was to snap back that at no point had I ever asked anyone questions that had anything to do with the murder. I was simply a listener.

'Understood,' I said meekly.

# Chapter 31

'Hi there. Looks like you've got us again for dinner this evening,' I said as the waiter pulled out the chair for me to sit down.

We'd sat with Susie and Jeff the week before. They were a friendly couple, and we spent a pleasant evening chatting. Towards the end of the meal, a chef, easily identified by his tall white hat, passed our table carrying a cake with several lit candles.

'Someone has a birthday,' said Susie.

We all turned to look.

'Is that David and Gwen?'

'Can't quite see.' Graham shifted in his chair. 'Yes, I think you're right.'

After we'd finished coffee, we said goodnight to Susie and Jeff and went to follow them out.

'Just a sec.' I put a hand on Graham's arm. 'That *is* David and Gwen. Shall we just go over and say happy birthday before we go?'

'You kept that quiet,' I said to David. 'We had no idea it was your birthday.'

David gave an embarrassed grin. 'I don't know who told *Sea Dream*, but the cake was a big surprise.'

'You have to put your date of birth on the booking form and the ship always likes to make a bit of a fuss. At least it's not like on some of the bigger glitzy cruise lines where they have all the waiters doing a conga behind the chef all through the tables singing 'Happy birthday' at the tops of their voices.'

'Thank goodness for that. That's not the only surprise gift I've had today. My lovely wife here, has given me a ticket for Silverstone and booked me a drive in an F1 car around the racetrack.'

'It very nearly wasn't a surprise.' Gwen gave a rueful chuckle. 'The envelope fell onto the floor when we were in the Wheelhouse Bar last week. I was worried David might see the logo on the front of the envelope.'

'I thought you snatched it up pretty quickly.'

Gwen grinned.

That evening, we decided to go to the theatre. The show cast were doing another of their special productions based on numbers from popular musical theatre ranging from *Les Misérables, Phantom of the Opera, the Lion King* and *Cats.* The voices of the four young singers blended well together and the dance group, three girls and two very athletic young men, performed their routines with gusto. How Mona would have loved it!

I blinked back the tears and forced myself to think of something else. Quite why Gwen's reaction when the envelope had dropped on the floor sprang to mind, I've no idea. What if the incriminating document that Doreen had got hold of was a letter? That was hardly likely to have come from someone she'd met on board. It was possible for someone to have dropped an envelope which Doreen picked up, but why would anyone be so careless with something they wanted kept secret? The most likely explanation was that it came from one of her own family. From what little I knew of her, the irascible woman always so quick to find fault was quite capable of finding ways of making people dance to her tune. I'd already considered Doreen as a blackmailer once. Not for money but power. Was that the reason for the escalation of hostilities between Doreen and her son-in-law? Sam had talked about her attempts to poison his relationship with Julie by suggesting that he was having an affair with a work colleague. Sam had flatly denied it, but that didn't mean he was telling the truth. It seemed perfectly possible that Doreen might go through his coat pockets while the couple were visiting and come across a love letter from his mistress.

If she showed it to Julie, it would be the end of their marriage. It was in the woman's character to dangle that possibility as a threat to keep him in line. It was easy to picture a scene with him pleading for its return – Doreen's derision driving him to distraction – her turning away to get in the lift – and finally, his lashing out in a moment of rage.

That scenario might explain Doreen's death. But why kill Mona? I had no idea what had happened to Mona so it was impossible to speculate, but while Doreen's death might well have been provoked, I could think of no explanation for Mona's death than as a deliberate murder. But what was the motive? I could just about picture Sam driven to extremes where Doreen was concerned, but what possible reason could he have for eliminating Mona? I liked the man. I felt sorry for him. Had I been deceived by a cold-blooded killer? Was I really such a bad judge of character?

It was late when we left the theatre. Far too late to seek out DCI Jarret. Was it worth taking my wild imaginings to him in any case? I had no proof. Best to sleep on it and think about it again in the cold light of the morning.

# Day 19

At Sea

# Chapter 32

We woke to an overcast sky and the view from our balcony was bleak. Dark grey seas broken only by the odd white crest of a wave stretched into the distant horizon to meet a gloomy solid sky only a few shades lighter. Where was the heatwave Britain had enjoyed the week before?

'Give it time. It's still early. Perhaps it will improve later.' Graham, ever the optimist, bent down to put on his shoes.

I picked up the *Cygnet Daily*. 'Not according to the forecast shown here. On the plus side, the lack of sun will probably drive everyone inside, so you may get more people to come to your lecture.'

'There is that I suppose. Are you ready to go up for breakfast?'

I ran the hairbrush through the tangles, picked up my cruise card, plastered a smile on my face and turned to face him. 'Aye, aye, Captain.'

I hadn't mentioned my encounter with DCI Jarret to Graham nor my musings about Sam as the culprit. Nor did I intend to. It wasn't easy to push away all thoughts of working out what I was going to do, and keep up a jocular mood. The last thing I needed was to let Graham think I was brooding over something. Graham's lecture wasn't until after lunch which meant that he would probably want some time alone in the cabin after breakfast to take a look through his presentation. My dilemma could wait till then.

It wasn't easy to find a quiet spot. All the lounges were filled with the noisy hum of chatter and even the library seemed to have attracted more people than usual. In the end, I curled up on the padded bench in the window on a corridor leading to one of the speciality restaurants pretending to read my Kindle. At this time of the day, I was unlikely to be bothered by too many passers-by.

It didn't take too much deliberation. There were holes in my theory, but it was possible that DCI Jarret knew nothing about Doreen's accusations about Sam's infidelity and for that reason alone it was best to go and speak to him. If he thought my idea of a love letter was the product of an over-active imagination, so be it. He was too much of a gentleman to laugh in my face.

I knocked tentatively on his office door. There was no answer. I tried again more firmly. Still no reply. There was no one in the corridor, so I risked opening the door. Empty. After taking so long to build up the courage and rehearsing exactly what I would say, I felt cheated.

A thought struck me as I trudged back to the Atrium Lounge. Perhaps the reason why DCI Jarret was not in his office was because he had solved the case and was even now in the process of arresting someone. In which case I would be spared from trying to convince him of my wild theory.

Graham had finished his practice session in time for us to go to the theatre for the morning lecture. It was David's last photography presentation and as I predicted first thing, the grey skies appeared to have helped swell the audience. We were among the last to arrive and the only seats available were right at the back.

On the way out we bumped into Paul and Margaret.

'That was a great lecture, don't you think?' I said as the queue shuffled slowly along the corridor.

'The content was good, I'll grant you, but the man really needs to do something about his diction. It's a well-known fact that the Birmingham accent is the least attractive in the country. The man needs to invest in a few voice classes.'

Several people turned to stare at us and even Graham frowned.

'Not everyone has the benefit of being born into well-educated middle-class home in the suburbs,' I snapped.

He glowered at me. 'I'll have you know; my father was a market trader in the East End of London. I've had to work hard to get to where I am today.'

He thrust his way through the crowd ahead and disappeared into the distance with Margaret desperately trying to keep up.

'It wouldn't have been so bad if he'd trashed David's presentation in private but to do so in a voice loud enough for so many passengers to be able to overhear was just unprofessional,' Graham muttered as we mounted the stairs.

'He was hardly any more generous about Sybil.'

Graham gave a wry laugh. 'Makes you wonder what he's said about my talks behind my back.'

The red light on the phone was blinking when we got back to the cabin. It flashed through my mind that it might be a message from DCI Jarret. I dismissed it immediately. What possible reason could he have for wanting to speak to me? Perhaps it was because I'd just been wondering how I could find an opportunity and speak to him without letting Graham know what I was up to.

'Looks like there's a message for you,' I said.

Graham walked over to the dressing table and pressed the button.

'Hi. This is Kirsten with a message for Graham. Sorry to drop this on you at the last minute but I want to have a very short meeting with all the lecturers in the wardroom at one o'clock. Thank you. Bye.'

'It better be short. I'm supposed to be in the theatre at half past to set up for my lecture,' he grumbled.

'I'm sure she appreciates that. She has to be there to introduce you.' I glanced at my watch. 'It's still a little early yet, but I suggest we go up for lunch when the Ocean Café opens at twelve to give ourselves plenty of time. You will need to change into your suit and get all your stuff together to take down with you so that you can go straight into the theatre at the end of the meeting.'

Secretly I was rather pleased Graham was going to be busy. It gave me the chance to see if DCI Jarett was back in his office.

The door was ajar. Not enough to see inside but enough to suggest that the chief inspector had returned. I was about to knock when I heard his voice. At first, I thought someone else was in there with him until I realised, he must be on the phone.

'Excellent…Give me the name again…Email me the details ASAP…Thank you.' There was a clunk as the receiver was dropped back onto its stand.

The door swung further open when I knocked. I could see him standing with his back to me, a pen still in his hand. He turned with a look of surprise on his face.

'The door was open,' I said, feeling the need to defend myself.

'The phone was ringing as I came down the corridor. I can't have shut it properly.' He looked and sounded a great deal happier than yesterday.

'Are you any closer to an arrest?'

'I don't know about that. I'm still chasing up reports from back home.' He picked up the pad he'd just been making notes on and walked round his desk back to his chair.

'You are obviously very busy, and I won't keep you. Last night I had this wild idea. I've been wondering whether to even bother you with it, but it is based on something you may not know, so I thought I'd come and run it by you anyway.'

'Shut the door and pull up a chair.'

'This rift between Doreen Bowland and Sam Rider.'

I told him about Doreen's accusation that Sam had been

unfaithful and then went on to tell him my suggestion of the possible sequence of events involving a stolen letter and blackmail.

'When I spoke to Mr Rider, he freely admitted that he did not get on with his mother-in-law and he told me about the argument the two of them had in the Atrium Lounge. He was upfront about how he lost his temper and actually said something along the lines of one day he would swing for her. He didn't mention any allegations about him having an affair. I admit there is a certain credibility to your idea but…'

'I know the whole idea is full of holes,' I interrupted. 'Not least that no one writes love letters these days. It's all texts and photos by phone. But if Sam was the one who broke into the Bowland's cabin, it would explain how he managed to get hold of the keycard so easily. Bill would have had no qualms about handing it over especially if Sam volunteered to fetch something from the cabin while Bill was still in the medical centre downstairs. He could even have got the code for the safe in the same way.'

'True. But why would Sam Rider have messed up the room? Surely, he could have made a thorough search without anyone else ever knowing.'

'The only explanation I can think of was that he wanted to throw suspicion on someone else. But the biggest argument against the whole idea is that though I can see how Doreen might have provoked him to lash out at her, I cannot come up with any reason why he would kill Mona.'

He sat back in his chair clearly deep in thought. The silence dragged on until he said, 'I admit I hadn't considered the scenario you described. You've given me a lot to think about but, as I'd been about to say earlier, the problem is finding any evidence to prove it.'

'But what about Mona? As far as I know Sam didn't even go ashore in Qaqortoq. He can't have been responsible for her death.'

He shook his head. 'I think it would be a mistake to assume that the two deaths were at the hand of the same person.'

'But surely, they have to be connected?'

'Not necessarily.'

He clearly knew something I didn't. Something he had no intention of telling me. He was back in official mode. He picked up his pen.

'I do appreciate you sharing your theory, but I do have a great deal I need to get on with.'

I was not going to be fobbed off so easily. 'You may not yet have a post-mortem report, but you must have a good idea how she died.'

'I'm afraid I am not at liberty to share that with you.'

'You asked for my help. Surely, I'm owed that much.'

He put down the pen and looked straight at me.

'However harsh this may sound; I am bound by police regulations. Technically, you are an informant not a colleague.'

# Chapter 33

Deep down, I knew he was absolutely right, no question. But nonetheless, despite his apologetic smile and the attempt to soften his words with the over-used platitude, what he had said was like a barb that pierced deep into my ego. Every cell in my body cried out for me to solve the mystery and be able to present him with a *fait accompli*. Did I really think that without all the backup – the forensic analysis, access to experts and background checks available to the police – and no previous experience in handling a murder enquiry, I could possibly discover the identity of Doreen Bowland's murderer? And as for Mona's death, I had absolutely nothing to go on. Not only that, I had no idea where to begin looking for evidence.

It was probably a good thing that Graham was already busy setting up for his lecture by the time I arrived in the theatre. At least I didn't have to put on an act to cover up the way I was feeling. When he came down from the stage, he went to talk to the passengers sitting in the audience until Kirsten came and the two of them stood by the steps waiting for the house lights to go down.

Needless to say, the lecture passed me by. Loath as I was to forget about the two murders and leave everything in the hands of the chief inspector and his team back at HQ wherever that was, what choice did I have? My only option was to try to put it all to the back of my mind and make an effort to enjoy the last few hours on board.

Or was it? What was it that Mona had said about seeing

someone who reminded her of some petty criminal from her past? I was rushing off at the time and we never finished our conversation. Looks can change considerably over the years. Could whoever Mona had seen in the Ocean Café really be the same person?

I was probably clutching at straws.

A couple of stagehands carried two heavy armchairs to the front of the stage while Graham was packing away his laptop. Even before he'd reached the bottom of the stairs down into the auditorium, someone else had whisked away the podium behind the curtain and out of sight into the wings.

'What's going on?'

'There isn't going to be another lecture this afternoon. Kirsten is interviewing the captain in the theatre at three thirty,' said Graham as we walked together to the doors.

He laughed as he saw the expression on my face. 'I presume you'd like to give that a miss?'

'Let's just say that I am not the captain's number one fan.'

'She'll be opening it up to questions from the audience at the end. You could aways go along and bowl him a couple of googlies.'

My shoulders began to shake, and I couldn't stop the bubble of laughter as I thought of the consternation that would break out if I demanded to know what he was doing about the murder of two of his passengers and how soon did he anticipate that the murderer, who must still be on board, would be apprehended. 'I could, but then you would never ever be invited to speak on any cruise ship again.'

'Best not then. So, what do want to do with the rest of the afternoon?'

'Cup of tea while we have a think. And you can tell me all about that last-minute meeting you had with Kirsten.'

He gave a snort. 'She wants us all in the wardroom at seven o'clock this evening in our best bib and tuckers so the photographer can take pictures. Partners included.'

'Couldn't she have just sent you all an email?'

'That's what several of the others said. To be fair, there were some other bits and pieces. A few last-minute changes to tomorrow's programme and to warn us there may well be a delay getting off the ship in Southampton. But that's strictly hush-hush and we're not to say anything to the passengers until a public announcement is made.'

'Did she say why?'

'Nope. Tony asked her, but all she said was that it may not happen anyway. I don't think she knew either.'

I heard the sob just before I turned from the corridor onto the landing. A blonde-headed woman was coming up the stairs. It was only when she glanced up that I recognised that it was Julie. Though, in that brief instant, I doubt she recognised me through her tear-filled eyes. Head down, she tried to hurry past me, but I put out an arm to stop her.

'Julie, what's wrong?'

She shook her head and tried to sidestep me.

'You're not going anywhere, until you've told me what's happened,' I said gently.

She covered her face with her hands and began to shake with silent sobs. I put my arm around her and led her back to my cabin. We sat side by side on the bed until the tears eventually subsided. Only then did I release my arm.

'Is it your father?'

She shook her head and pulled another fistful of tissues from the box I'd placed beside her.

'You don't have to tell me, but it might help to get it off your chest.'

'Sam's been gone all afternoon and now they're searching our cabin. They won't tell me what's happening.'

'Why don't we start at the beginning? Where is Sam now?'

Brushing away the last of her tears with the back of her hand, she took a deep breath. 'Dad said he was tired when we came back for lunch, so I took him back to his suite for him to have a lie down. It took a while getting him settled, drawing the curtains and making sure he had everything he might need by the bedside. When I went back down to our cabin there was a note on the bed from Sam saying that he'd been asked to go down to the security office. I waited for an hour, but he didn't come back.'

Another tear rolled down her cheek. I thought for a moment that she was about to burst into tears again, but she took a deep breath to steady herself and continued, 'I went to look for him, but I couldn't find him. I didn't know what to do. He's still not back. I think he's been arrested. They're searching our cabin for drugs.'

'Is that what they told you?'

'Not exactly. Three officers arrived and one of them asked me if Sam had ever taken drugs. I told him the whole idea was ridiculous, but they insisted on searching the cabin. They are taking it apart. They even took out all the drawers and turned them upside down to see if there was anything taped underneath. When they lifted the mattress off the bed, there wasn't room for the three of them and me in the cramped space, so I left. But now I'm worried that I should have stayed. What if they plant evidence on him while I'm not there?'

'I honestly don't think they are likely to do that. Why on earth would they want to frame Sam?'

She was quiet for a long time.

'He has been acting different since Mum died.'

'It must have been a shock for all of you.'

She shook her head. 'He and Mum never got on.'

'I think he was upset because he felt guilty about the argument the two of them had just before she died, and that you blamed him for your mother's death.'

'I suppose I did for a while, but that was just the grief talking. We made it up again.'

'It probably didn't help that you had to spend so much time looking after your father especially after he fell down the stairs. Sam was left on his own to brood for long stretches of time.'

197

She shrugged. 'It probably didn't help that the security people kept asking us all sorts of questions for days. That's probably why he got this weird conviction that Mum was murdered. They were back again asking more questions this morning. That's why we were so late going for lunch.'

'What did they want to know?'

'They kept asking about what we were doing when we went ashore, where we went and who we spoke to, did we see anyone else from the ship, that sort of thing. It was odd, none of us could see the point.'

'It does seem a little strange,' I lied. I had a good idea of what DCI Jarret had been trying to establish.

'I better be getting back to my cabin. See if they've finished. It's going to take ages to get it back to rights after the mess they're making.'

'I'll come back with you and help.'

Not that help was needed. We arrived to find the cabin steward putting the final touches of making the bed of an otherwise tidy room.

My mind was working overtime as I made my way back to my own cabin. DCI Jarret had certainly not wasted much time before interviewing Sam Rider after our discussion. Whether that meant he gave credence to my idea or was he checking a lead of his own, was anyone's guess. Was the phone call he'd taken as I had arrived significant? A new lead perhaps? This was the first time I'd heard mention of any interest in drugs. Logic said that ship security would have an ongoing interest in ensuring that no drugs ever came on board although I had never noticed any indication that any special searches were made.

Not for the first time, I fervently wished I could discuss everything with Graham. Having to explain everything to him would clarify my jumbled thoughts.

I'd considered it odd that Jarret was so pedantic when I'd used the word fun-loving to describe Mona. Was he trying to establish if she was a drug user? In all honesty, I had to admit that I could just about picture her as the type who might indulge in recreational drugs at wild parties in her youth perhaps forty or fifty years ago, but not now. And the idea of her looking to find a supplier while she was in Qaqortoq was ludicrous. Even more unbelievable was the idea that she could be a dealer.

# Chapter 34

'Formal nights are bad enough without having to have our pictures taken as well,' Graham muttered as he tried for the third time to sort his bow tie.

'Don't be such a grouch.'

'Says the woman who scowls whenever I try to take a photo of her when we go out.'

'That's because you always want to take it when my hair's all over the place or I'm bundled up in a padded jacket and look like a female version of the Michelin man. I've never understood this obsession everyone has these days for selfies in front of historic buildings or whatever.'

'It's to prove they've actually been there.'

'That's my point. All the photo shows is a closeup of someone grinning inanely and you can't see what's in the background anyway.'

'Now who's the grouch?'

He took his jacket off the back of the chair and slipped it on. 'Are you ready?'

We were among the last to arrive. There was a waiter just inside the door holding a tray of glasses. I declined the fizz and took a glass of orange. This was probably going to be a long night and no doubt we would be plied with drink at the start of every course, of which there were always a good half-dozen on formal nights.

We mingled with the crowd which included not only the lecturers but the craft and art instructors and the chaplain, plus all the partners. A large mottled blue backdrop had been set up against one wall plus a couple of large white reflectors on either side sectioning off an area for the photos. The wardroom is relatively small and the poor waitresses serving canapes had a difficult job weaving through the clusters of people.

After a few minutes, Kirsten clapped her hands for silence.

'I think we're all here now. Good evening, everyone, and thank you for coming. The captain will be arriving shortly to say a few words, but I just wanted to give my own sincere thanks to each and every one of you. You've been a great group of people to work with and I've heard nothing but praise from our passengers about the lectures and the workshop sessions. So, ladies and gentlemen, I'd like you all to raise your glasses and toast what has been an excellent cruise and, just in case I don't get to speak to you personally again, here's to the next time I see you back onboard with us.'

The next twenty minutes were spent with each couple having their photos taken. The photographer must have taken half a dozen pictures of Graham and me with us arranged in different positions, some formal and others less so. It was then time for the group photos.

First up were the lecturers and craft leaders.

'We'll have the three women on chairs in front with the men standing behind,' said the photographer.

As everyone moved into position, Kirsten looked around. 'That's not right. Someone's missing. Where's Tony hiding? Come on Vicar. You're included. No point trying to hide at the back there.'

Tony, dressed in clerical grey and dog collar, looked even more reluctant to have his photograph taken than Graham and I had been earlier. Come to think of it, I don't remember him taking his turn earlier when the single photos were taken.

As the photographer spent the next few minutes

rearranging positions to create a symmetrical top line, something Mona had said about the man from her past came back to me. Though our conversation had been cut short and she never told me his name, she had said it wasn't a passenger. Did "one of your lot" imply it was a lecturer?

David was standing at the end of the row. As far as I knew, David and Mona had never met. Certainly, neither had mentioned the other. Nor had David had any direct confrontation with Doreen Bowland. Though DCI Jarret had said it might be a mistake to consider both women died at the hand of the same person, I was convinced the two deaths had to be connected. Was I being swayed by the fact that I liked the self-effacing rather shy photographer? Even pleasant, likeable normally Godfearing individuals can be driven to do unexpected things in extreme circumstances.

Standing next to him was Philip Tomlin, the art instructor. I knew absolutely nothing about him and had never spoken to him. Nor could I imagine a scenario where he and Doreen would ever come across each other's path.

That brought me to Paul. By his own admission, he had dragged himself up from an unpromising start in life. But there was nothing to indicate that his current more-than-comfortable state was the product of crime rather than sheer determination and hard work. It would be a mistake for me to let my dislike of the man cast him in the role of Mona's petty crook. The man was a misogynist, and he gave every indication that he had a temper, but even I had to admit, that was a far cry from labelling him a murderer.

Passing over Graham, that left only Tony Parker-Scott. The main problem with him was that he wasn't a Londoner. And when all was said and done, he was a vicar!

Any further musing on my part was interrupted by the arrival of the captain. He gave a short predictable speech of thanks to everyone saying how the lectures and various activities were a vital part of what made Cygnet Cruises so successful and how we had all contributed to make this one of the best yet.

Graham and I exchanged glances. Memorable, certainly, but we both knew the captain would be more than happy to see the back of this one.

One last group photo was taken with the captain, and we all filed out to make our way to the Italian Restaurant. Sybil and Genevieve walked in front of us. Sybil was looking none too happy, and I caught snatches of their conversation.

'Don't be such a killjoy. Cheer up, big sis. It won't be that bad.'

'As long as I don't have to sit next to that man. There's definitely something of the night about him.'

I wondered who she was talking about. Paul and Margaret were just ahead of the couple, and I wondered if he had said something to offend Sybil and decided it was more than likely.

Once we arrived in the restaurant, Kirsten led the way to a long oval table at the far end large enough to seat all fourteen of us.

She stood behind the chair at the head of the table and announced, 'Let's mix things up a little. No husbands and wives sitting next to one another. You'll see enough of each other when you go home the day after tomorrow, so I want you all to take a place next to someone you haven't had a chance to chat with up till now.'

I found myself between Sylvia the craft instructor and Tony Parker-Smith on the end of the table. Opposite me, on Tony's left was Gwen with Philip the art instructor, a man I'd never spoken to before, next to her. At least sitting at the curved end of the table I would have three or four people that I'd be able to talk to with ease. Graham was halfway down where the table had widened out which meant he only had the people on either side he could chat to. Much to my surprise, I noticed that Sybil and Paul were next to each other. Perhaps he was not the man with something of the night about him that she'd been referring to.

Silence descended on the whole table as everyone studied

the menu. I didn't think I could manage all seven courses, so I declined the salad, the fish course and the cheese and biscuits though I did opt for the sorbet before my Tortelli con zucca, which according to the waiter, consisted of pasta stuffed pumpkin, crushed cookies and parmesan cheese.

Sylvia was the first to start up the conversation. 'Has everyone enjoyed the cruise?'

There were nods and murmurs of agreement all round.

'And what has been the best bit for you?'

'My favourite port was Reykjavik,' said Philip. 'Don't get me wrong. Greenland was fascinating and I'm delighted to have been there. The scenery was mesmerising, like nothing I've seen anywhere else. We were so lucky to be able to get into all four ports, but, if I'm honest, it's not top of my list of places to go back to, whereas I'd love to return to Reykjavik. There are still so many things there I'd like to see and do.'

I nodded. 'I know what you mean. We were so fortunate that all our foggy days were when we were at sea. The weather couldn't have been better. And there were a couple of trips I won't forget in a hurry. The one to the foot of the glacier in Narsarsuaq was exhilarating and the visit to a local home in the last port was a great insight into a very different way of life.'

'We were so lucky,' said Sylvia. 'If you take a look at the videos on YouTube, lots of cruises have problems with mosquitos but I only ever saw a handful of our lot ever bother putting on the nets we were given.'

'If you can manage without, why bother? You can't see properly with all that thick black net draped all over your face. They ruin the view,' said Philip.

'I had hoped to bring back a few nice souvenirs from Greenland and I was a little disappointed with the lack of shops,' said Gwen. 'How about you, Tony? Are you a shopper? I saw you come back on board with a rucksack stuffed to the gills when we came back from Kirkwall.'

Tony's eyes widened in surprise, then he gave a chuckle.

'I'm definitely not a shopper. I visited an old mate of mine in Kirkwall, and he gave me a few presents to take to some mutual friends back home. And to answer your other question, I think my favourite part of the cruise was the day we spent sailing through Prince Christian Sound. Seeing all those icebergs up close and the glaciers above us was something I'll never forget.'

'Oh yes. That was very special,' agreed Sylvia.

The waiter arrived to take our orders and there was a lull in the conversation.

I was talking with Sylvia, so I didn't catch the start of the discussion between Gwen and Tony, but I gathered she'd been asking him about where he was living back home because I heard him say, 'I was in a country parish. I'm on a sabbatical at the moment. Having a few months leave before taking up a new appointment.'

'My brother is a clergyman. He was moved last year from a busy city parish to one in the country. He's finding it a big contrast. His parish covers several villages, so he seems to spend half his time in the car travelling to conduct services for ever declining but very devoted and demanding congregations.'

Tony gave an indulgent smile. 'It can be a problem.'

'I expect you're missing your old parishioners, aren't you? Where were you exactly?'

'North Yorkshire. Holy Trinity in Skipton.'

'What a coincidence,' I said joining the conversation. 'Graham and I are thinking of taking a holiday up in the Dales in a place just outside Grassington. I expect you know it well.'

'Not really. My duties didn't leave a great deal of time for sightseeing.'

'We've never been to that area before. You and I must have a chat sometime about the places you would suggest we visit.'

'Tomorrow perhaps.' His expression was unreadable. 'Ah good. Here come our starters and I need some more wine.'

The rest of the evening passed pleasantly enough, though I probably drank far more than I should have done. Each course came with its own wine and though I insisted on only half a glass each time, I'll swear the wine waiter managed to keep topping it up when I wasn't looking.

It was long gone ten o'clock before the party broke up.

'Much to my surprise, the evening went quite quickly,' I said once Graham and I were out of earshot.

'Lucky you!'

'Oh dear. I take it you didn't enjoy it?'

'I had Margaret on one side and the wife of the art chap on the other. Every time I tried to start up a conversation, neither could manage to string together more than half a dozen words. It was damn hard work; I can tell you.'

'At least you have to admit that the food was good.'

'That I'll grant you. Though why they decided to put caramelised pears with the Florentine beef steak, I'll never know.'

'You should know by now every dish has to have some fancy addition to be considered haute cuisine. Like the baked figs that came with the duck yesterday. I'm only grateful that I don't have to cook a meal or wash up afterwards. Enjoy it while you can because it's back to sausages and baked beans the day after tomorrow.'

'Actually, after all this rich food at sea for three weeks, I'm quite looking forward to some simple home cooking.'

'Hey. Not so much of the simple thank you, or you'll be doing the cooking as well as wiping up!'

I removed my necklace and matching earrings and went to put them in the safe. Graham keeps his spare camera lens in there and I had a job finding my jewellery box. As I was rummaging in the back, one of the passports fell to the floor. I bent to retrieve it and I suddenly recalled the last time I'd picked up a passport. A passport that didn't actually belong to the woman who dropped it.

'Something wrong?'

'No.' I shook myself out of my reverie. 'Just thinking

about something that's all.'

# Day 20

At Sea

# Chapter 35

The curtains were already drawn back when I opened my eyes to see a cloudless azure sky outside. I had no idea what time it was, but I was happy to lie there in a half-doze. After a stressful few days, I felt entitled to a lazy start.

I heard Graham padding around trying not to wake me. Perhaps it was time to get up. I rolled onto my back, stretched out and opened my eyes again. He came round to my side of the bed then bent down to kiss me.

'Happy anniversary, darling.' He whisked out a card from behind his back and laid it on my chest. 'I'm afraid I couldn't arrange for Interflora to deliver you a bouquet this year. Apparently, they don't do helicopter drops at sea anymore, and the shop downstairs doesn't sell flowers. However, on the plus side, I am going to take you out for a posh meal upstairs tonight.'

'Cheapskate.' I laughed, put my arms round his neck and pulled him down for another kiss. 'To be honest, I hadn't realised the date.'

'You mean, you forgot again.'

'No! I do have a card for you somewhere. That's if I can remember where I've hidden it.'

I never forget birthdays – they are marked in my diary in any case – but our wedding anniversary has crept up on me unawares a couple of times before.

I sat up, arranged the pillows and opened my card. It was a soppy one with two teddy bears sitting on a park bench beneath a heart-shaped moon. Inside he'd written, "To my darling wife. You still look as beautiful as you did when you walked down the aisle forty-two years ago."

'If only,' I chuckled. 'Forty-two years! Where have they gone?'

I put the card on my bedside table and went to throw back the duvet.

Graham put out a hand to stop me. 'Tell you what. You stay there and I'll make us both a cup of tea and we'll be really decadent and drink it in bed. I don't have any more lectures today so there's no need to rush up to breakfast. It's going to be all go tomorrow when we get back to Southampton, so let's have a lazy day.'

My heart sank. Comments like that had a nasty habit of tempting fate and after what I had discovered yesterday, the chances of having a lazy day looked a remote possibility.

'Sounds good. But first, while you put the kettle on, I need to find the card I brought for you.'

I pulled out the largest suitcase from under the bed. One of the big advantages of a no flying cruise is not having to worry about a weight limit and with twenty-two days at sea, I'd brought plenty of clean clothes. The disadvantage is there isn't enough drawer space to put everything so the rest of it is left in zip-lock bags in the case. I'd hidden the card in the middle of a pack of my underwear, the one place I knew Graham wouldn't come across it accidentally. I stood there chewing my bottom lip as I stared down at the card in my hand.

'Something wrong?'

I looked up and smiled. 'No. Just thinking.'

I laid the card on Graham's side of the bed, resealed the plastic bag and got back on my knees to put everything away again.

'I think I might just see if I can find Richard Jarret a bit later on.'

'Mr. Brown Suit? What on earth for?'

'I'm still worried about Mona, and he's the only one who's likely to tell me if there has been any news.' It wasn't exactly a lie, but if I told him the whole truth, he'd only tell me not to interfere.

Sybil was waiting by the rotary toast machine when I went up to the counter. She turned and smiled.

'I noticed you drew the short straw last night having to sit next to the high-and-mighty Reverend Parker-Scott.'

I smiled. 'Do I take it from that remark that Tony is not your favourite person?'

'Can't stand the man. Thinks far too much of himself. Any man who dyes his hair is suspect in my opinion. Smacks of vanity.'

'Does he dye his hair? I hadn't noticed.'

'How many fifty-year-olds do you know without a single white hair? He's supposed to be a clergyman, for goodness' sake. Though, in my opinion, anyone less like a man of the cloth would be hard to find.'

'Why do you say that?'

'For a start, he knows damn-all about theology and anyone who confuses Westminster Abbey and Westminster Cathedral, even if he did correct himself when he saw my reaction, shouldn't be in the job. A genuine Anglican priest would never make that mistake in the first place.'

We chatted on for a moment or two until her toast was done and it was my turn to pop bread in the toaster.

Graham had almost finished his cereal by the time I got back.

'You've been gone ages.'

'There was a queue. While I was waiting, I had a chat with Sybil. She was having a rant about Tony.'

'What did he do to upset her?'

'Heaven knows.'

'I think I might go and see if I can find a free lounger up on the sun deck a bit later. It's a glorious day.'

I raised an eyebrow. 'Good luck with that. I bet half the ship has the same idea.'

'You're probably right. Still, it's worth a try.'

'Does that mean you're going to skip the lecture this morning?'

'Not sure. I need to clean my teeth and collect something to read anyway, so I'll come down with you to the cabin and see what the subject is. What are you planning on doing?'

'I should make a start on the packing.'

'Sure you don't need any help?'

I shook my head. 'It's easier if just one of us does it. There's not enough room with two of us at the same time.'

Not that wrapping up shoes and sorting out dirty washing was at the top of my to do list for the morning. Graham had given me the perfect opportunity to seek out DCI Jarret and try to make him listen to my latest ideas. But first I needed to check something with Julie. Though how I was going to be able to track her down was another question altogether.

# Chapter 36

It was still far too early for coffee so there was little point in searching all the lounges on the off chance of running into Julie and Sam. There was a good chance that Julie had started packing. Although I'd been to her room only the day before when I'd offered to help tidy up after it had been searched, it hadn't occurred to me to make a note of the number. I knew it was halfway along the long corridor just before the laundrette. Though logic said it was probably next door to one the Bowlands had occupied, the tape and do-not-enter sign had long been removed. I narrowed it down to three or four.

I knocked on the one I thought the most likely. The door opened a crack and a disgruntled looking woman, her hair still uncombed, peered round it.

'I'm so sorry. I've obviously got the wrong room. I don't suppose…' The door slammed shut before I had a chance to finish my sentence.

After that experience, I decided I'd had enough of banging on doors. The receptionist had refused to give me Mona's cabin number so there was little point in trying to persuade anyone on the desk to help.

Julie had mentioned that Bill had been moved to a suite at the top of the ship. I had no idea how many suites there were. Presumably not many. Perhaps I could find a helpful cabin steward to point me in the right direction.

There were no more than a dozen cabins on the top deck and to judge from the distance between the doors, four appeared to be larger than the others, but there was little evidence of any cabin stewards around. At this time of the morning, at the very least, I'd expected to find a trolley laden with clean towels and sheets sitting in the corridor.

As I stood there trying to decide what to do next, I heard voices from one of the cabins and a door opened. A woman emerged in an over-sized towelling robe clutching a large blue swimming towel.

'I wonder if you could help me.' I gave her my best smile. 'I'm trying to find Bill Bowland's cabin. Do you know which it might be?'

'It's the one next door. Bill always has room service for breakfast so he may not be up yet, but I expect his daughter's in there now. She usually pops up about this time to check on how he is.'

She bustled off along the corridor before I had time to thank her.

I stood at his door for a moment trying to decide what to do. There was no guarantee that Julie was in there and the last thing I wanted was to make him have to get out of bed if he was alone. I double-checked the corridor was empty and put my ear to the door. Not that it did any good. I wasn't sure I'd be able to hear anything anyway.

Feeling dejected, I made my way back to the stairs. As I turned onto the stairwell landing, I almost bumped into someone coming out. We apologised simultaneously and as I took a step to the left, she moved right. We did that silly little dance from side to side until we both stood still and smiled at each other. Only then did I realise that it was Julie. She had considerably more colour than the last time I'd seen her, but that may well have been because of the flights of stairs she'd just climbed.

'How goes it?'

She grinned. 'Much better than when I saw you yesterday. Sorry I got a bit hysterical. Heaven knows what you must think of me.'

'I'd have been in a state too if I'd been in your place. I take it that Sam's back safe and sound?'

'Yes. Thank goodness. They gave him a right grilling though. Asked him if he'd ever taken drugs. He's no angel, but he'd never do anything that stupid. He was a bit of a tearaway when he was a teenager. He was even taken to the police station with a crowd of other lads after they got drunk in a pub and got chucked out for rowdy behaviour. Half of them were underage including Sam. He got a good telling off, but he was never charged. Back then, lots of the boys in his class regularly went into pubs. No one bothered to ask your age or demanded to see ID.'

'I'm glad everything's been sorted.'

'Yes, thank goodness. I was just going to see how Dad is and sort out his packing. Then I suppose I ought to go and check if it's alright to pack up Mum's things. I can't do that until they let me have a key. Since that intruder broke in, none of us have been allowed to go in there except when we had to check to see what was taken.'

'Did they ever find out why he did it?'

'No. It's a mystery. Why go to all that trouble and not steal anything? They didn't even bother with the cash.'

'Very odd. One last question. Sam mentioned your mother had an argument with another passenger at security the day you got on the ship. Do you know what that was about?'

'That seems a lifetime ago now. As far as I can remember, one of the x-ray machines went on the blink and several people had to have all their hand luggage gone through by one of the staff. It caused a bit of a hold up. The chap in front of Mum had to empty out his backpack. The trays were backing up and mum wanted to get at hers and pulled her tray further down. It knocked into this other chap's and all his loose stuff fell off into her tray. He wasn't best pleased and said something to upset Mum and there was a bit of a scene.'

'Do you know who the man was?'

'No idea. I don't think I've seen him on the ship since.'

'Can you describe him?'

'Not really. I was trying to see to Dad, so I wasn't paying much attention. Mum wasn't exactly the easiest person to deal with when she was in that mood. I just let her get on with it.'

'This man was he young or old?'

'About my age I'd say. Late forties. Perhaps a bit older. Why do you want to know?'

'Just curious. Anyway, I mustn't keep you. If I don't see you again, take care.' It seemed crass to wish her all the best knowing the shock that she and the family would face when they learnt the truth about Doreen's death and have to endure all its consequences.

'Bye and thanks for all your support. Sam and I really appreciate it.'

We gave each other a brief hug before I hurried down the stairs feeling a fraud and a coward even though I knew there was nothing I could say to warn her of the anguish that lay ahead for all the family.

# Chapter 37

My problems weren't over. I would need every ounce of courage I could muster to tackle my next task. The sooner I faced DCI Jarret the better.

Despite all my misgivings, luck must have decided to do me one good turn. There was no need to knock on his door. He was standing in the doorway of the security office almost opposite his own talking to someone inside. I covered the remaining distance before he'd noticed my approach.

The moment he turned, I said, 'Did you make a full security check of the Bowlands' room after the break in?'

'Why would we?' Just as I'd hoped, he was so surprised by my question, he'd answered before I'd given him time to protest at my invasion.

'In which case, if you get a passkey to their room, I'll show you where to find what the intruder was looking for.'

He stared at me for a moment attempting to reassert his authority. 'Mrs Mitchell, would you care to explain what all this is about?'

'If you come with me, I'll show you.'

Leaving him no time to argue, I turned and started to walk towards the stairs, crossing metaphorical fingers in the hope he would follow no matter how exasperated he was becoming.

As I climbed up the three double flights of stairs, I slowed my pace to give him time to collect the keycard and catch me up. I didn't want to have to hover in the corridor not knowing which room I was heading for. It was a relief when

I heard his hurried steps behind me. I stood to one side to let him lead the way.

He turned to face me as he held open the door. 'If you are wasting my time, there will be consequences.'

Julie had mentioned that the cabin steward had put the room to rights by the time she gone to collect her father's things to take up to his suite. Her mother's clothes were now folded and lay in neat piles on the bed. I was not the only one who followed the advice given on various holiday websites and travel magazines about packing your clothes into see-through bags.

Several empty bags sat on the dressing-table, but much to my relief, there were still a couple of bags the intruder hadn't bothered to empty – one of socks and stockings and the other of underwear. Neither bag was bulky. Once he'd picked it up, it would have been obvious to the intruder that there could be nothing else hidden amongst the spare footwear. The second bag held a week's worth of knickers and uncomfortable looking bras, plus an enormous corset.

I picked it up and slid the underwear onto the bed, holding my breath. The corset was stiffened with whalebone or more probably its more modern equivalent.

'I didn't think it was still possible to buy this sort of thing,' I said more to myself than to Jarret. 'This type went out long before my time, but it obviously made a perfect hiding place.'

I withdrew my hand from inside, clutching what I could now see was a passport. I handed it straight over to DCI Jarret. 'I think you'll find this is what your intruder was looking for.'

I perched on the end of the bed looking up at him with a smug grin plastered on my face.

'Well, I'm damned.'

He turned to the identification page. Even upside down I could see that the man in the photograph had fair hair with a neatly trimmed beard streaked with grey, but I couldn't read the name.

Jarett pulled his mobile from his pocket and crossed to the balcony doors. Whether that was to get better reception or to prevent me from listening in to the conversation, I had no idea.

'I'm holding a passport in the name of Clive Steven Colebrook…'

His voice dropped even lower, but I'd caught the name. There was something about it that jogged a memory. I was so wrapped up in my own thoughts that I was only dimly aware that Jarret had finished his call and was now standing a few feet away staring at me intently.

'Do you have something else to tell me?'

'I presume you were asking your people to do a check on the passport's owner. I suggest you ring back and ask them to send you all they have on the Reverend Anthony Parker-Scott at the same time.'

His eyes narrowed. 'I think you had better come with me.'

# Chapter 38

Ten minutes later, we were down in his office. He took the chair behind the desk, and I pulled the only other chair from against the wall and sat facing him. He laid the passport on the desk then sat back, his elbows resting on the arms of the chair, and steepled his fingers. His expression was unreadable and the way his eyes held mine made me intensely uncomfortable.

'Would you care to tell me exactly why I should ask members of my team to go scouring through records for details of a respected Church of England clergyman vetted by Cygnet head office?'

'Is there a real Reverend Parker-Scott? When you say vetted by Cygnet head office, what does that mean exactly?'

'As I understand it, the company has a list of clergymen they can call upon. The list is made up of individuals who are recommended by existing members. Parker-Scott has been in the ministry for twenty years and the vicar of a Yorkshire parish for the last seven. He was invited to join Cygnet Line almost a year ago. He was offered a place on a cruise over Christmas, but he was taken ill at the time and had to decline it. If I remember correctly, this is the first cruise he has been able to do since his recovery.'

My throat went dry. I licked my lips and took a deep swallow. No turning back now. 'I have no doubt that the real Parker-Scott was as estimable as the cruise line considered him to be, but I believe there is a strong possibility that the man now posing as ship's chaplain is in reality a certain Clive Steven Colebrook.'

'And on what evidence have you come to your conclusion?' The sarcasm in his voice was readily apparent.

'On the basis of the sheer number of admittedly small but significant things that have come to light. The Reverend Parker-Scott may well be a country vicar based in Skipton, however when I mentioned we were thinking of going on holiday to Grassington, the man calling himself Tony Parker-Scott claimed he'd only visited the village a few times. Yet when I was researching the area on the internet for our holiday, I discovered that Holy Trinity in Skipton is the nearest church. There is less than ten miles between the two. Grassington is part of his parish so the real Parker-Scott would have been a frequent visitor to conduct services. Plus, according to Dr Sybil Adams, Tony knows nothing about theology. Part of her first degree was in Divinity.'

'And what makes you believe our Parker-Scott is Clive Steven Colebrook?'

'I'll admit, that is just a hunch. According to Tony, he had a cousin named Clive who died three months ago in Switzerland, but what if it was the other way round? It was Parker-Scott who died. It would explain how our man got hold of the genuine passport. If the two were cousins, there could well be a strong enough family resemblance for him to get away with it. Let's face it, most of us don't look that much like our photos. And why else would our Parker-Scott have Clive's passport?'

'We can soon find out.' He picked up the phone and punched in a number. It was answered straight away. 'I need an up-to-date check on the Rev. Anthony Parker-Scott…That's the one…anything in the last year…Could you send it over as soon as you can. Thanks, Mike.'

He put down the receiver, looking thoughtful, then turned back to me.

'Even if what you claim is true, how on earth did Clive Colebrook's passport manage to end up in Doreen

Bowland's possession?'

'There was a confrontation between her and a dark-haired, middle-aged passenger while they were passing through security to get onto the ship. How many other passengers have you seen on this ship that fit that description? Cygnet Cruises leaving from British ports have always tended to attract older guests who don't like flying. Especially when they provide an included taxi service from their home to the port which cuts out a great deal of the hassle of getting to the ship. The altercation started when several of Parker-Scott's belongings fell from his tray into hers. In all the confusion, I believe the passport was mistakenly left behind which is how Doreen came to get hold of it. When he discovered it was missing and realised what must have happened, he probably went to ask for it back. From what I saw of Doreen, plus her reputation, it's not difficult to imagine her response. Even if by then she had found it, she was the type who'd want to make him suffer by holding on to it until much later in the cruise.'

'Let me get this straight, you are suggesting that Parker-Scott stole the handbag and when he discovered his real passport wasn't in there, approached Doreen Bowland a second time and demanded it back? The two had another heated argument and he hit her and killed her intentionally or otherwise. Then still unable to retrieve the passport, he broke in to the Bowland's cabin to look for it.'

'That's exactly what I'm suggesting.'

He sat tapping his steepled index fingers on his chin. 'But why would he bring the passport on board with him in the first place?'

'I agree. That little conundrum kept me awake until the small hours this morning. The only thing I can come up with is that it was left in one of the multitude of pockets in his rucksack and he only found it when the x-ray machine went on the blink, and he was made to empty the whole kit and caboodle to be inspected by hand. Either that or he needed to prove his identity for something else. Apart from it having to do something with drugs, what I can't explain is why he had to kill Mona.'

At the mention of the word drugs, the detective's eyebrows shot to his hair line.

'What do you know about drugs?'

'Isn't that why Clive was posing as a clergyman on board? When he found the invite from Cygnet for the Rev. Anthony Parker-Scott to join the cruise, he would have jumped at the chance. What better way would there be to move drugs from one country to another? No one would suspect a clergyman.'

'You are making a great many assumptions. How would he have got them through all the checks at Southampton?'

'He didn't. That's how the whole operation works. Once you get on board in the first place, it's a whole lot easier. Still risky, but not impossible. I presume he collected them when he went ashore in Kirkwall when he told everyone he was visiting an old friend. I know he came back to the ship with a full rucksack. If he timed it right, when several tours were returning and the queues were backed up, he could have sneaked past the ship's security machine somehow.'

Jarret's eyes narrowed, but he said nothing.

'I saw him myself in Qaqortoq when he was going into a house with one of the locals. At the time, I thought he was on one of the local visit tours. It didn't strike me until now that he could have been delivering drugs. He said himself that he never went on any of the tours when we were in port. If he were dropping off the drugs to local dealers in each port that might well explain why.'

Jarret's mobile buzzed and he picked it up. 'Hi, Mike. That was quick.' He listened for a few moments. His eyebrows shot towards his hairline. 'Many thanks. I owe you one.'

He pulled his laptop towards him and opened it up. Clicked few more keys, then read aloud, 'On the 28th of February, the Rev. Anthony Parker-Scott entered a sanitorium in Switzerland but discharged himself two weeks later. Clive Steven Colebrook went missing when out skiing while on holiday in Davos on the 1st of April. His body was never recovered but one of his skis was found near a crevasse off-piste.'

I said nothing but it was an effort to stop myself from jumping up and punching the air in jubilation.

'There's a couple of photos here. What do you think?'

I stood up and walked round the desk to look over his shoulder. Parker-Scott's smiling portrait in clerical robes, presumably taken soon after his ordination showed a much younger man, with a round baby face which bore an obvious resemblance to that of the grim-faced man in the obvious police picture alongside identified as Clive Steven Colebrook. Apart from the colour of his hair, the second man was clearly our Tony Parker-Scott.

Jarret sat back and gave a heart-felt sigh.

'I thought you'd be elated.'

'The passport confirms our suspicions, but it still isn't evidence. I don't have enough to charge him.'

'But he murdered two people.'

He shook his head. 'The local police are only prepared to say that Mona Etherington's death is suspicious. Her body was found in a disused fish factory at the bottom of a waste chute. She could have been exploring and fell.'

'That's rubbish. Mona had no sense of direction and was terrified of getting lost. She never went ashore alone and even when she went on a ship's excursion, if the group was given free time, she'd ask to tag along with other people.'

'But why would Clive Colebrook have any reason to get rid of her?'

'I've been thinking about that. At the start of the cruise, she and Tony seemed to hit it off, then for no apparent reason, Tony started avoiding her. We both assumed that was because he was worried about his image as ship's chaplain if he was seen to be paying a great deal of attention to one of the lady passengers. Especially one who liked to let herself go in the late-bar drinks and dancing. But, just before she disappeared, she talked about seeing someone on the ship who bore a marked resemblance to this petty criminal who used to hang around with an East End mobster.'

To say that DCI Jarret looked sceptical was putting it mildly. 'I think you're beginning to let your imagination run away with you. Are you saying Mrs Etherington was a member of a criminal gang?'

'No! That's not what I'm saying, at all.' My fingernails bit into my palms. I took a deep breath. 'It's too long a story to explain. Mona and I were interrupted, and she never told me who this person was, but after what we've just discovered, what if was Tony, and when she saw him in Qaqortoq she challenged him?'

Jarret's mobile gave a second strident burble. His eyes widened as he glanced at the name of the sender. I beat a hasty retreat back to my chair. He pressed the accept button and put it to his ear, 'Sir.'

He listened for a few seconds, then said, 'Just a moment, sir. I have someone with me.'

He looked across at me. I took the hint and left closing the door quietly behind me.

It was frustrating to say the least.


I knew I was on the right track, but how could I prove it?

I stood in the empty corridor trying to come up with some way of finding out if anyone had seen Mona and Tony together that morning. Suddenly, I had an idea and hurried round to the starboard side of the ship. As luck would have it, Liam was at his desk.

'Sorry to pester, but can you tell me who escorted the town walk and museum excursion in Qaqortoq?'

He looked at me dubiously, 'Not offhand.'

'I can see you're busy, I wouldn't ask but it is important.' I gave him my best smile and pleading look.

He grinned. 'As it's for you, I'll look it up.'

He clicked away at his keyboard then stared at his monitor. 'There were three walking tours that morning.'

'The one that left at nine o'clock.'

'Then that would be Gwen Cox.'

'That's great. Liam, you're a star!'

There was a good chance she would be in her cabin busy packing. As I should be, I thought ruefully.

'I know this might seem an odd question, but do you remember a woman in an emerald green padded jacket with a fur hood when you were escorting the walking group in Qaqortoq? She was quite a chatterbox.'

If she was surprised at my question, Gwen didn't show it. 'Yes, I do. Nice lady. She was going to come back to the ship with me at the end of the trip but then changed her mind at the last minute.'

'Do you know why?'

'I presume she went to look at the rock carvings on the cliff face just above where the tenders came in. The guide said they were well worth looking at, and there was a circular path that took you up there.'

'Did you see her with anyone else?'

'She was a friendly soul and chatted with everyone.'

'I meant at the end. Someone who wasn't in your group.'

'Not that I noticed. Though there were several groups coming back at the same time as ours. To be honest, I didn't pay much attention when she left as there was a tender loading up and I didn't want to miss it.'

'I see. Thanks anyway.'

'Sorry I couldn't be more help.'

'I'll let you get back to your packing.'

# Chapter 39

Graham's packing lay in neat piles beside the empty case open on the bed. He was on his knees in front of the French window arranging shoes and assorted clutter into the grip.

'Sorry, sorry, sorry. I know I said I'd do the packing, but I decided to have a quick word with Richard Jarret to see if he could give me any news on Mona before I made a start. I met Julie on the way, and we had a long chat. Then it took a while to find Jarret. Did you go to the lecture?'

He stood up and turned to face me. I'd expected him to be annoyed and start asking difficult questions. Though that might well have been better than the look of disappointed resignation he gave me instead.

'I see you've made a good start on the packing. I can do the rest.' I slid open the wardrobe door. 'Have you had a coffee yet? I could certainly do with one. Could you be an angel and pop along to the library and get me one from the coffee station while I get cracking?'

'Amanda love, stop. There's no need for the act. We've been married for far too long for me not to know that you've been keeping secrets from me since the day you found that woman's body in the lift. Come and tell me what's gone wrong now.'

I still couldn't turn and face him. I banged my fists on the wardrobe door. 'I'm just so bloody angry.'

I felt his hands on my shoulders gently turning me round until I was in his arms, my head buried in his chest. He held me close as I fought to calm my frustrated nerves.

Eventually, my pounding heart rate returned to something more like normal. I put my hands on his chest and tried to push away. He loosened his grip but kept his hands locked round me.

'It's all so wrong,' I muttered. 'After all that effort and finally tracking down the killer, it looks as if he's going to walk free.'

'Killer? I thought you were worried about Mona.'

For the first time I looked up into his face. 'Oh, Graham. I wish I could tell you everything and the moment we get back in our car at Southampton and start driving back home, I'll tell you every last detail from the very beginning, I promise.' I managed a weak smile. 'It's a long story. It'll probably take the whole journey anyway.'

'Fine. But leave the packing for now. Let's both go to the library for that coffee, find a comfy sofa and we can talk about what we're going to do when we get back to celebrate our wedding anniversary because, let's face it, today hasn't exactly been a raging success.'

I stood on tiptoe, took his face in my hands and kissed the tip of his nose. 'Great idea. But let me just go and comb my hair and make myself presentable.'

After lunch, my resolve had strengthened. I wasn't prepared to sit back and do nothing. I would tackle Jarret again. He would probably refuse to see me, but I would make him listen even if I had to threaten to tell everyone on the ship what had been going on.

I knocked, and without waiting for a reply opened the door, and marched across to his desk.

'You weren't surprised when I mentioned drugs this morning. You knew all about drugs being on board the ship. It's why you had Sam Rider's cabin searched. Did you already know Clive Colebrook was posing as Tony Parker-Scott and that he was the one who brought them on board in the first place?'

'No.' He banged his fist on the table and jumped to his

feet. He recovered quickly and sank down back into his chair.

'I knew cruise ships were being used to bring in and distribute drugs, but I had no idea that was happening on this ship.'

'So is Clive now under arrest?'

He shook his head.

'Why not? Surely, you've searched his room. Even if he's already delivered the last of the drugs, what about all that cash he must have received in exchange?'

'I sent someone as soon as you left this morning. It was clean.'

'Then presumably you'll be able to arrest him when he tries to leave the ship, tomorrow morning. He's not going to leave it behind. He's bound to have it with him then.'

He sat back saying nothing. His face looked pained.

'Well?'

He rubbed his face in his hands.

'I'm not leaving this room without an answer.'

He let out a long sigh. 'I shouldn't be telling you this. Colebrook is a bit player in a major syndicate. The drug squad have been after them for nearly a year. They want to catch the major players and close down the whole operation.'

'So you're saying, Clive Colebrook is going to be allowed to just walk off this ship.'

'Knowing the runner's identity will give the squad an advantage when the organisation repeats the scam.'

'Are you really telling me that you are just going to sit back and let a murderer walk free?'

'*I* am not in a position to do anything. That phone call I had this morning when I asked you to leave was from the top brass. My request for a search on Clive Steven Colebrook triggered an alarm. I am to back off. It's out of my jurisdiction. Whatever my feelings on the matter, I have my orders. The drug squad boss trumps my boss.'

'Whatever happened to justice?'

'Believe me, I'm as angry as you are. But I have to face facts. You and I may be convinced that Colebrook is a murderer, but I just don't have any hard evidence to prove it. As things stand, my boss wouldn't let me take a murder charge to the CPS anyway. The case would be thrown out of court on day one.'

'There must be something you can do.'

'I've tried everything I could think of. We've searched his room for blood-stained clothes, but he either stuck them in the launderette, threw them overboard or dumped them when he went ashore because we've searched the whole damn ship. There's no sign of whatever he hit her with either. And as for Mona Etherington, the Greenland police can give me nothing.'

We sat in silence as the minutes ticked by.

There was nothing more to say.


By mid-afternoon, our cases were more or less packed apart from the last few bits and pieces.

'I shan't bother getting glammed up for dinner tonight. Everyone else will probably change into the clothes they're going home in tomorrow. I might as well pack away all my make up now and stick it in the grip.'

I unzipped my makeup bag and dropped in all the lipsticks and eyeshadows that were sitting on the shelves beside the bathroom mirror over the sink. I'd treated myself to an expensive bottle of liquid foundation just before we'd come away and before putting it with the rest of the stuff, I made sure the top was properly screwed on. The last thing I wanted was for the viscous liquid to leak over everything and make a mess. There was already a rim of solidified goo around the neck of the bottle. I unscrewed the lid and wiped around the top of the bottle with a wet tissue. My hands must have been wet too because the bottle slipped from my fingers and crashed onto the floor. Luckily, the glass didn't break but liquid spewed from the bottle in a great arc across the floor as it fell. I swore.

'What's happened?' Graham was at the door in seconds.

'Don't come in,' I yelled. 'If you tread in it, it will get everywhere.'

I stood staring down at the mess. My brain working overtime.

'What's wrong?'

I shook my head. Decision time.

'I need to find DCI Jarret right now. Don't bother about this mess. I'll clean it up when I get back.'

I'd gone before Graham had time to protest.

To my immense relief, he was still sitting there when I burst in.

'Did you check the soles of his shoes?'

'I beg your pardon?'

'You said you'd checked Tony's room for blood-soaked clothing.'

He nodded. 'According to the doctor, the wound was relatively small. Whatever he hit her with was blunt. It crushed the skull and most of the bleeding was internal. The ship's doctor is not a trained pathologist, but he thinks there would probably have been a fine spray over the killer's clothes but nothing major. There was a small amount of blood and a trail on the carpet from when she was dragged into the lift. Most of the blood on the back wall seems to have oozed out after she was propped against it, which suggests she didn't die straight away.'

'Once the heart stops, the blood stops pumping.'

'Exactly. So, what's this about the shoes? There were no blood-stained shoes in his cabin if that's what you think. As I said, there probably wasn't a lot of blood splatter. Not enough to cover his shoes.'

'Not the tops admittedly. But, if he'd stepped in the blood when he was dragging in the body and propping it, there would be traces however small. If traces of her blood are found on his shoes surely it must count as evidence.'

He chewed his bottom lip. 'Great idea but it would take

days for the results to come through.'

'I realise that, but perhaps that's not necessary. You can test for blood.'

'Mrs Mitchell, Amanda. If I arrest him on that evidence, I could kiss goodbye to my job.'

I shook my head. 'But if he confesses to the murder, you will have no choice. You would be duty-bound to arrest him. From what you told me, Clive Colebrook is not a major criminal. He's simply a petty crook paid to deliver drugs and bring back the proceeds. From what I know of the man, he is a vain poser, and he's certainly not the brightest boy in the class. If he was, he'd have done his research a great deal more thoroughly and he certainly wouldn't have got drunk in the all-night bar and made an exhibition of himself. If you flatter him and ask him to meet you somewhere private – not a formal interview in your office or across in security obviously, just a friendly encounter – you'd be able to spring all the stuff you now have on him. Sit him down, sweet talk him then confront him with the bag of underwear. When you pull out that corset, I'll guarantee you'll get the same reaction I saw on your face when I did it. Then you produce the passport. Build up the pressure. Then produce the shoes. That's when you play your sympathetic card. You know he didn't mean to kill her, but she drove him to lash out…'

He raised a hand. 'Are you telling me how to do my job?'

'Not at all. I'm just visualising how you would go about it. I know from experience how your gentle approach is far more intimidating and likely to get results than the belligerent aggressive style the security officer comes out with.'

'So, it's flattery now.'

I couldn't stop the girlish giggle. 'Anyway, I'll leave you to it. I've got a bathroom floor covered in makeup to clean up.'

He raised an eyebrow.

'Don't ask. Good luck.'

I turned and fled before he could say any more.

# Chapter 40

I felt as though a great weight had been lifted from my shoulders. The whole thing was far from over and there was probably only a fifty-fifty chance that DCI Jarret would be able to pull it off, but at least I had done as much as I could. I'd never spoken to Doreen Bowland and from what I'd learnt about her, I confess my determination to track down her killer was prompted more from the realisation that the same man must also be responsible for Mona's death.

Unless Clive Colebrook owned up and revealed the details, there was a good chance that no one would ever know what led to Mona being killed, and there was no way that I would ever get to hear how the friendly woman who had been so full of life met her end. *Rest in peace, dear Mona, wherever you are.*

Graham had already cleaned up the bathroom floor by the time I got back, despite what I told him.

'I take it things went well?' he said.

'The final result is yet to come, but let's just say, I'm considerably more hopeful than I was this morning.' I quickly changed the subject. 'It's only just gone four o'clock. How about we go to the restaurant for afternoon tea? It's the last chance we're going to get on this cruise.'

'Your wish is my command, m' lady.'

Lots of other people seemed to have had the same idea because the restaurant was heaving when we got there. We hovered in the entrance while the waiter attempted to find us a couple of empty seats. Eventually we were led to a large table in the centre already occupied by three other couples who appeared to be either close friends or family and had come as a group. After a brief greeting, they resumed their conversation, saving Graham and me the need to make small talk. It was sometime before we were brought a cake stand with its three tiers of assorted savouries and cakes.

'Any chance of a cup of tea?' Graham smiled up at the waitress.

'I'll send someone over.'

Usually there were several waiters with large pots of tea and coffee circulating around the room offering a top-up, but I had seen no one in our vicinity since we sat down.

'I don't hold out much hope. Perhaps this wasn't such a good idea after all,' he muttered.

'Oh, ye of little faith,' I chuckled. 'At least we are going to get a scone. I spy a waiter at the table behind you.'

I'd already polished off a smoked salmon and cucumber finger sandwich and an almond macaroon and was ladling a generous dollop of clotted cream on top of my fruit scone by the time the tea arrived.

Our table companions had already finished and were joining the ever-increasing flow of people leaving the restaurant long before we'd finished eating.

'I'm not leaving till I've had a second cup of tea.' Graham waved at a couple of waiters standing at one of the serving stations and lifted his cup and saucer.

'I'll have another one as well, please,' I said, when the young man arrived. 'These dainty cups don't hold nearly as much as the mugs we have at breakfast.'

I sat back cradling my cup in my hands when I spotted Sam, Julie and Bill making their way out. I caught Sam's eye and waved. All three turned and waved back. Sam said something to the others then came over.

'Just come to say goodbye and to thank you. You'll never know how much your kindness meant to me that first time you spoke to me in the library. I was so wretched. It was as though the whole world was against me. Just knowing someone cared made me pull myself together.'

'Don't mention it. What time do you get off tomorrow?'

'They are going to take Doreen's coffin off the ship first thing once the port authorities have given permission for the ship to disembark, which will probably be round about five thirty and we'll be leaving with it. It's going to be a difficult day for all of us. Bill's agreed to come and stay with us for a couple of weeks before anything else is decided. We have no idea as yet as to when the police will release the body so we can't make any arrangements for the funeral.'

I pushed the chair back and stood up to give him a hug. 'You are all in my prayers.'

'Thanks.'

He turned and hurried away.

I stared at his retreating back. It was a good thing they had each other for support in the hard days that lay ahead.


'What time are we allowed off in the morning?'

Graham picked up the *Cynet Daily*. 'Says here that the first to leave the ship are those allocated green luggage labels at eight o'clock. As we're responsible for taking our own cases off, we can leave any time after that.'

'But didn't Kirsten say the other day that disembarkation could be delayed?'

'You're right. I'd forgotten that. There's nothing on the sheet to indicate that.'

'I suppose we'll have to wait until tomorrow and listen out for any announcements.'

There was a knock at the door.

'I'll go,' I said.

The last person I expected to see was DCI Jarret.

'May I come in?'

'If you don't mind the mess.'

There wasn't a lot of space with the cases stacked against the wall and our hand-luggage dotted all over the cabin.

'Do you want me to disappear while you speak to Amanda?'

'No, that's fine. I'm not stopping.' Jarret turned to me. 'I just thought you might like to know that Clive Colebrook has been arrested and charged with the murder of Doreen Bowland.'

'Did he confess?'

Jarret nodded.

'What about Mona?'

'I'm working on that, don't worry. One step at a time. I didn't want to leave without thanking you for your keen observations.'

'I'm not sure I was much help really. You'd worked out most of it long before I started pestering you. You'd have got there without me.'

He smiled. 'Probably. But at the end, you did help speed up the process. Anyway, I won't keep you.'

He held out a hand and we shook hands.

'Thanks for letting me know.'

I closed the door and turned to face Graham who was staring at me with a bemused expression.

'Are you allowed to tell me what the heck is going on? Who on earth is Clive Colebrook?'

'I don't suppose it would hurt for you to know now it's all over, but you are not to even hint to anyone else. Not now and probably best not in the future either. Clive Colebrook is the real name of our Reverend Anthony Parker-Scott.'

'Tony! A murderer?'

His reaction made me laugh. 'Let's clear the armchairs and sit down and I'll tell you the whole story from the beginning.'

# Day 21

*Today we return to port.*

*Captain Jonathan Clarkson and his crew would like to thank you for joining us aboard* The Sea Dream, *and trust you had a memorable and enjoyable time with us. All of us at Cygnet Cruises wish you a safe journey home and we hope to see you again in the near future.*

Extract from the Cygnet Daily

# Chapter 41

The alarm on Graham's phone went off at six o'clock. I dug an elbow in his back.

'Switch it off. That music gets on my nerves.'

I hate waking on the alarm, but two minutes under the hot shower had me feeling considerably livelier and I felt ready to face the day.

We were up in the Ocean Café soon after half past. As I'd anticipated, it was busy. Although the departure time for many people wasn't until well into mid-morning, everyone had to vacate their cabin by eight so that the stewards could get the rooms cleaned for the next set of passengers coming aboard.

One of the waiters was wiping down a table by the window so I hurried over to claim it while Graham went to the buffet. I looked out of the window, staring down at the quayside. A large white van closely followed by a black taxicab was slowly pulling away from the cargo gangway on the lower deck.

'I've just seen the mortuary van leaving,' I said softly to Graham when he got back.

Breakfast at home for me was a slice of toast. I can't remember the last time either of us had had a cooked breakfast. Probably not since our camping days when the children were small. Even onboard ship, though I occasionally have scrambled egg on toast, I never go for the full English with all the works. On a fly cruise, when I know I won't be getting any lunch and we won't be home until late, I always promise myself I'll treat myself to a decent cooked breakfast. More often than not, by the time we get to the dining-room, I just can't face a big meal so early in the day.

After such a long cruise, I fancied a change to my usual selection. I walked the length of the buffet counter trying to decide what to have. Seeing the mortuary van had quite taken away my appetite. I was so busy looking at what was on offer and lost in my own thoughts that I almost bumped into someone waiting to be served.

'I'm so sorry. Oh hi, Margaret.'

''Morning, Amanda.' She seemed a lot brighter and cheerful this morning than I seen her all cruise.'

'Happy to be going home?'

'I am rather. Three weeks is a long time to be away and I'm missing my cat. Not that I haven't enjoyed the cruise.'

'It's certainly been interesting.'

She laughed. 'Eventful you might say, what with people dropping dead with a heart attack and a break in. Did you know that some policemen came on board when we arrived?'

'Really?'

'I didn't actually see them, but when I went out on to the balcony first thing there was a police car on the dock just below our cabin.'

'Perhaps it was security officers doing a routine inspection. I expect it often happens.'

She looked quite deflated. 'Do you think so? I've never noticed them before.'

'That woman's only happy when she has some juicy gossip to spread,' I said, as I put my plate on the table with more force than I'd intended.

I relayed what Margaret had told me.

'I'm amazed you managed to get a conversation with her at all. I think the woman must be frightened of men. The day we sat at her table for breakfast when we were in

Reykjavik, she scuttled off the moment you left the pair of us together. And then at the celebration dinner, I don't think she strung more than three words together the whole evening. I take it you didn't tell her the real reason they came aboard.'

'Certainly not. Anyway, we don't know that uniformed officers actually boarded the ship. Somehow, I can't quite see a passenger being handcuffed and marched off the ship between two burly policemen. Cygnet Cruises would never live it down. Can you imagine all the Tweets and pictures plastered over social media? I expect DCI Jarret whisked Tony off the ship through the cargo gangway away from prying eyes and escorted him to the waiting police car.'

'No sign of any police cars on the dock now,' I said, as we wheeled our cases across the short gangway to the zig-zag skyway that led down into the terminal building.

There we collected a trolley, loaded our cases and backpacks, and headed for the exit. The carpark was just across the road from the terminal. Graham collected his car keys from the man in the kiosk and by a quarter to nine we were in the car and ready for the drive home.

'Bye-bye *Sea Dream*,' I said, as I craned forward to look up at the looming ship.

'Apart from all the drama, did you enjoy the cruise?' Graham asked.

'Yes, very much. I enjoyed all the ports and the scenery. I'll never forget sailing through Prince Christian Sound and all those glaciers. I'm glad we went and that we've seen Greenland, but I don't think I'm that keen to go a second time. Too many bad memories.'

Graham chuckled. 'Okay. So what would you like me to put down on my request form for future cruises? Anywhere in particular.'

'Not especially. It's your choice after all. You are the one who has to do all the work and prepare all the lectures. I just have to sit back and enjoy the holiday. That said, I'd rather you choose one where there isn't going to be a murder on board.'

He laughed out loud. 'I'll do my best, sweetheart. But no promises.'

# ABOUT THE AUTHOR

Judith has three passions in life – writing, travel and ancient history. Her novels are the product of those passions. Her Fiona Mason Mysteries are each set on coach tours to different European countries and her history lecturer Aunt Jessica, accompanies travel tours to more exotic parts of the world.

Born and brought up in Norwich, she now lives with her husband in Wiltshire. Though she wrote her first novel (now languishing in the back of a drawer somewhere) when her two children were toddlers. There was little time for writing when she returned to work teaching Geography in a large comprehensive. It was only after retiring from her headship, that she was able to take up writing again in earnest.

Life is still busy. She spends her mornings teaching Tai Chi and yoga or at line dancing, Pilates and Zumba classes. That's when she's not at sea as a cruise lecturer giving talks on ancient history, writing and writers or running writing workshops.

\*\*\*

*Find out more about Judith at www.judithcranswick.co.uk*

Printed in Great Britain
by Amazon